HUMAN RIGHTS AND MEMORY

ESSAYS ON HUMAN RIGHTS

EDITED BY THOMAS CUSHMAN

This series features important new works by leading figures in the interdisciplinary field of human rights. Books in the series present provocative and powerful statements, theories, or views on contemporary issues in human rights. The aim of the series is to provide short, accessible works that will present new and original thinking in crystalline form and in a language accessible to a wide range of scholars, policymakers, students, and general readers. The series will include works by anthropologists, sociologists, philosophers, political scientists, and those working in the more traditional fields of human rights, including practitioners.

Thomas Cushman is Professor of Sociology at Wellesley College. He previously edited a series for The Pennsylvania State University Press titled Post-Communist Cultural Studies, in which a dozen volumes appeared. He is the founding editor of two journals, Human Rights Review and the Journal of Human Rights, and he now serves as Editor-at-Large for the latter. He is a Fellow of the Yale Center for Cultural Sociology.

ALREADY PUBLISHED:

Bryan Turner, *Vulnerability and Human Rights* (2004)

Keith Tester, *Humanitarianism and Modern Culture* (2010)

John Rodden, *Dialectics, Dogmas, and Dissent: Stories from East German Victims of Human Rights Abuse* (2010)

Rhoda Howard-Hassmann, *Can Globalization Promote Human Rights?* (2010)

OTHER TITLES FORTHCOMING:

Nancy Tuana, *Global Climate Change and Human Rights*

DANIEL LEVY AND NATAN SZNAIDER

HUMAN RIGHTS AND MEMORY

THE PENNSYLVANIA STATE UNIVERSITY PRESS
UNIVERSITY PARK, PENNSYLVANIA

Library of Congress Cataloging-in-Publication Data
Levy, Daniel, 1962–
     Human rights and memory / Daniel Levy and Natan Sznaider.
          p. cm. — (Essays on human rights)
Includes bibliographical references and index.
Summary: "Examines the foundations of human rights, how their
political and cultural validation in a global context is posing challenges to nation-state sovereignty, and how they become an integral part of international relations and are institutionalized into
domestic legal and political practices"—Provided by publisher.
ISBN 978-0-271-03738-7 (cloth : alk. paper)
ISBN 978-0-271-03720-2 (pbk. : alk. paper)
1. Human rights—History.
2. Human rights—Social aspects.
3. International relations—History.
I. Sznaider, Natan, 1954– .
II. Title.

JC571.L49   2010
323—dc22
2010007051

The Pennsylvania State University Press is a member of the
Association of American University Presses.

For ELLA AND SHIRA

CONTENTS

ACKNOWLEDGMENTS

This book owes much to conversations with friends and colleagues. More than anything else it is the product of an ongoing exchange and research agenda that we started with Ulrich Beck in the late 1990s. Thus, the book is a constant intellectual engagement with his ideas and concepts. We have been drawing a great deal of inspiration from our conversations with him over the years.

We thank Tom Cushman for initiating this project and for his enthusiastic and sustained support throughout, which did not diminish his critical and incisive comments.

Thanks also to Sandy Thatcher and his staff at Penn State University Press. In addition, we thank Esther Singer for her editorial help. Thanks also to the anonymous reviewer for a close reading of an earlier draft and a very supportive endorsement.

Last but not least, we would like to thank our respective academic institutions, Stony Brook University in New York and the Academic College of Tel Aviv–Yaffo in Israel for granting us research leaves.

This book also presents results of our joint research project (funded by the Deutsche Forschungsgemeinschaft). It is a continuation of our earlier work, *The Holocaust and Memory in the Global Age* (Temple University Press, 2005), in which we developed the concept of "cosmopolitan memory." In the current book we expand upon a variety of themes that address the historical, political, and cultural connections between memory and human rights. We advanced some aspects of this link in an article entitled "Sovereignty Transformed: A Sociology of Human Rights," *British Journal of Sociology* 57, no. 4 (2006): 657–76. Our focus on Europe builds on our earlier essay "Memories of Europe: Cosmopolitanism and Its Others," which appeared in *Cosmopolitanism and Europe*, ed. Chris Rumford (Liverpool: Liverpool University Press, 2007). The politics of forgiveness is an elaboration on ideas we first articulated in "Forgive and Not Forget: Reconciliation Between Forgiveness and Resentment," in *Taking Wrongs Seriously: Apologies and Reconciliation*, ed. Elazar Barkan and Alexander Karn (Stanford: Stanford University Press, 2006).

THE UBIQUITY OF HUMAN RIGHTS
IN A COSMOPOLITAN AGE

> Once we had a country and we thought it fair,
> Look in the atlas and you'll find it there:
> We cannot go there now, my dear, we cannot go there now.

This excerpt from a poem by W. H. Auden, written shortly before the outbreak of World War II, is a poet's outcry for a more humane world, for a world without cruelty. It is a poet's wish that his words can make for a better world by displaying compassion for others. Today, this outcry is couched in the language of human rights, which seems to be everywhere. Human rights mean much to many, but also many different things. As a new universal language, they have been surprisingly underconceptualized. Are we talking politics? If so, what kind of political implications do human rights have? Or are we talking aesthetics, which implies a kind of "human rights experience" without a great many political consequences? This brings us full circle to the outcries of poets and intellectuals.

Nevertheless, there is agreement that human rights matter. Contemporary societies are suffused with images making just this point. Imagine yourself watching pictures on TV or on the Internet. They show brutal beatings, people being forcibly evicted from their homes, or soldiers assaulting innocent civilians parade before your eyes. This is no movie clip, but rather actual images from realities nearby or far away. What do we make of these pictures? Do we have a language that can make sense of them? *All human beings are born free and equal in dignity and rights. They are endowed with reason and conscience and should act towards one another in a spirit of brotherhood.* Thus states Article 1 of the Universal Declaration of Human Rights. These are noble words, but do they have political meaning, and, if so, what are their implications? Are they consequential?

The language of human rights provides us with a framework to begin to understand why pictures of strangers being beaten and tortured by other strangers concern us. Why do we care? Should we care? What is it about the power of human rights that makes us find these scenes revolting? Has this always been the case? If not, does this mean that our relation to human suffering, our passion for human rights, is not a given but is historically contingent? If so, what historical contingencies have made us more responsive to the sufferings of strangers? Human rights and allegiance to them is a rather recent phenomenon. Who can afford to be against human rights? At least rhetorically, human rights have become a kind of universal currency in politics. Clearly, this alone does not guarantee a world without violations. Even when viewed as simply a Western ideological move or just another sophisticated form of colonial imposition, human rights have turned into a global phenomenon that must be reckoned with. This book is an attempt to show how we reached this particular point in history.

One of the most serious obstacles to fulfilling the ideals of human rights is the proclaimed sovereignty of nations. Human rights declarations are formulated as a set of rules, regulations, and norms challenging sovereignty. The principle of "noninterference" in so-called internal affairs is exactly the opposite of the human rights regime,[1] which claims that there is no such thing as "internal affairs." When it comes to certain types of abuses, human rights are about humans and not about members of specific states. The end of the cold war in 1989 and the emergence of global interdependencies have highlighted the tensions between the imperatives of a human rights regime and the prerogatives of sovereignty.[2] This means that sovereignty—the prerogatives of the bounded state, the political community, the bounded "we"—has hitherto taken precedence over the unbounded universal "we."

With the fall of the "Iron Curtain," one of the most important divisions of the latter half of the twentieth century collapsed: the world was no longer split into the "free world" and "Iron Curtain" countries. This division, however, has been superseded by another dichotomy: those who violate human rights and those who do not. National and ethnic conflicts such as those in the former Yugoslavia and in the Middle East are being interpreted by a global audience as human rights problems rather than as existential and ethnic divisions. Attempts to reverse this development have had little impact on international politics. For instance, in his first response to the violent repression of the Tibetan opposition in the spring of 2008, Chinese president Hu Jintau unsuccessfully sought to sever the two, stating, "Our conflict with the Dalai clique is not an ethnic problem, not a religious problem, nor a human rights problem. It is a problem either to safeguard national unification or to split the motherland" (New York Times, April 13, 2008, 10). This attempt at suasion, which would have attracted scant attention in the first three postwar decades, did little to change the focus on human rights that dominated the media coverage of the Tibet protests, the ensuing calls to boycott the Olympic Games, and political leaders' decisions to stay away from the opening ceremony.

Human rights have become a principle of political legitimacy, inaugurating a new kind of politics (Forsythe 2000; Henkin 1999). Although the rights revolution of the past two decades has not always deterred human rights abuses, it has created strong normative and institutional foundations to penetrate the shield of sovereign impunity. Increasingly, compliance with a set of human rights norms—such as dignity and rights for all—is circumscribing the legitimacy of unacceptable state actions. Adherence to a minimal set of human rights ideals has become a significant, albeit uneven, factor in global politics and a prerequisite to preserving legitimacy (Rosas 1995).

One factor that has led to divisions between particular (national) identifications and universal (human rights) orientations is the decoupling of nationhood and state. The state is now considered a neutral institution that regulates the affairs of its citizens without necessarily providing them with a strong sense of belonging and identity. Clearly states have retained most of their sovereign functions, but the basis for their legitimacy is no longer primarily conditioned by a contract with a bounded nation. It is also determined by a state's adherence to a set of nation-transcending human rights ideals. Thus legitimacy is mediated by the extent to which states engage in or commit to an emerging human rights regime and an "internal" affair can easily become an "external" one.

How exactly does the relationship between human rights and sovereignty work in contemporary politics? Has the human rights regime become a parallel universe to the existing system of nation-states? What are the implications of these historical developments for the conceptualization of statehood and the balance of particular (national) identifications and universal orientations? In the following book, we will examine the link between human rights and sovereignty through the analytic prism of historical memories. Historical memories refer to shared understandings of and responsibilities for the significance the past has for the present concerns of a community. Through memory, a political community validates challenges and reproduces itself. More specifically, we argue that historical memories of past failures to prevent human rights abuses have become a primary mechanism through which the institutionalization of human rights idioms and their legal inscription during the past two decades have transformed sovereignty. The global proliferation of human rights norms is driven by the public and frequent ritualistic attention to memories of their persistent violations. The emergence of this global cultural "memory imperative" finds its expression in a set of political and normative expectations to engage with past injustices.

Historically, this is a European phenomenon that emerged against the backdrop of memories of World War II and the Holocaust (Levy and Sznaider 2001, 2005). Memories of the Holocaust have evolved into a universal code that is now synonymous with an imperative to address past injustices (both legally as well as in commemorative terms). Although the "memory imperative" originated with the centrality of Holocaust memories during the 1990s, it has by now become a decontextualized code for human rights abuses as such. Rather than challenge the primacy of human rights, most opposition to injustice is now articulated through the categorical denial and remedial efforts of rights violations instead of prospective visions for a just society. The victims of the present can no longer find salvation in the future but must be redeemed by connecting their experience to an iconographic past of human rights violations. Nation-states engage or are expected to with their own history in a skeptical fashion. This dynamic, we argue, explains both the importance of human rights norms as a globally available repertoire of legitimate claim making and the differential appropriation of this universal script.

We went to examine, therefore, how, at different historical junctures and through the proliferation of memories of past injustices, the discourse of human rights has evolved into a powerful idiom vested with legitimacy. We analyze how the discourse of human rights has developed into a cultural and political force that is substantially reconfiguring the basis of legitimate sovereignty, the scope of political responsibility, and forms of belonging. The accretion of political, cultural, and institutional capital in the form of a human rights regime has resulted in a substantial reconfiguration of state sovereignty extensions of political responsibilities, and the potential for extending forms of solidarity beyond the realm of nationhood. Rather than start from an abstract notion of political interests (grounded, for instance, in power or capital), we probe how, once institutionalized, human rights idioms themselves constitute political interests that shape power balances and, by extension, the contours of sovereignty and solidarity. Memory politics of human rights has become a new form of political rationality and a prerequisite for state legitimacy. Sovereign rhetoric is increasingly evaluated by the extent to which it is related to the legal recognition of human rights. Memory clashes abound and provide ample evidence that the prominence of human rights does not imply the end of the national and at times even raises the specter of renationalization or retribalization. However, the prevalence of human rights, the mediated proliferation of memories of human rights abuses, and their association with particularistic politics do signify the diminishing normative return of nationalism.

For a full grasp of the ways in which the contested relationship between sovereignty and human rights discourse unfolds, we thus bring two hitherto largely unconnected fields—namely, rights and memory studies—to bear upon each other. Our approach departs, however, from the otherwise nation-centric treatment of memory politics that is characteristic of the social sciences, where the nation and the state are frequently treated as interchangeable terms, thus masking the historically conditioned nature of political sovereignty. Contrary to conventional approaches that associate memory with national identifications, we argue for a cosmopolitan conception of memory that focuses on the simultaneity of universal and particular outlooks. We do not treat universalism and particularism as superior or inferior moral choices but rather look at them as modes of existence that can change over time. We historicize these notions, thereby de-moralizing them, while retaining them as valuable sociological tools. This has consequences for the study of memory. The cosmopolitanization of memories refers to practices that shift attention away from the territorialized nation-state and the ethnically bound frameworks that are commonly associated with the notion of collective memory (Levy and Sznaider 2001, 2005). Rather than presuppose the congruity of nation, territory, and polity, cosmopolitanized memories are based on and contribute to nation-transcending idioms, spanning territorial and national borders.

We consider the recent proliferation of human rights ideals as a new form of cosmopolitanism, exemplifying a dynamic through which global concerns become part of local experiences. The choice of "cosmopolitanism" as a new moral and political idiom in this connection is not arbitrary. It relates to political and intellectual forms predating the era of the nation-state. Crucially, it has resurfaced at a time when the basic premises of the nation-state have been challenged and the shape of its sovereignty is being transformed. Naturally, this does not mean that cultural and ethnic nations are merely illusions or that the identities they provide are nothing more than mistakes or delusions. If that were the case, the concept of cosmopolitanism would be no different from a reproduction of a virulent universalism.[3] Rather, we need to differentiate the social modalities that deal with difference, such as universalism, relativism, ethnicity, nationalism, cosmopolitanism, and multiculturalism. Universalism obliges us to respect others as equals as a matter of principle, yet for that very reason it does not involve any requirement that would arouse curiosity or respect for what makes others different. On the contrary, the particularity of others is sacrificed to a postulate of universal equality that denies its own context of emergence and interests.

We suggest a different approach to cosmopolitanism that is based on a "universalistic minimum" involving a number of substantive norms that must be upheld at all costs. These substantive norms include the sanctity of the body and the avoidance of unnecessary cruelty. We use the term "cosmopolitan common sense" when we have good reasons to assume that most individuals would be willing to defend this minimum (Beck and Sznaider 2006, 19). Therefore, our cosmopolitan reading of human rights is not part of a postmodern deconstruction of all master narratives—including those of human rights—but continues the project of modernity by retaining some of its normative quests for a better and a just life, the aforementioned sanctity of the body being one of them.

The turn of the twenty-first century has been marked by fundamental global transformations that challenge some of the paradigmatic assumptions of a methodological nationalism bound up with the presupposition that the "national" remains the key principle and yardstick for the study of social, economic, political, and cultural processes. The shortcoming of this perspective is not the predictable finding that national memories remain dominant, but rather the reluctance to problematize the concept of the nation itself. We do not question the continuous relevance of national orientations. The value of country-specific experiences does not consist of explaining how the national remains dominant, however, but instead how global referents (such as human rights ideals) are incorporated into the political-cultural scripts of nations.

In contrast to the normative universalism of the Enlightenment (Kant) or of the contemporary continuation of that project (see Nussbaum 2002), our analytic approach to cosmopolitanization refers to a process in which universalism and particularism are no longer exclusive "either/or" categories but instead a coexisting pair.[4] Following Ulrich Beck's definition of cosmopolitanization as "a non-linear, dialectical process in which the universal and particular, the similar and the dissimilar, the global and the local are to be conceived not as cultural polarities, but as interconnected and reciprocally interpenetrating principles" (2006, 72–73). We start our research trajectory with a critique of methodological nationalism.[5] This suggests a shift beyond a nation-state-centric methodology. In short, a critique of methodological nationalism in the context of globalization research demonstrates that a national ontology can no longer serve as a self-evident point of departure.

Our cosmopolitan perspective offers a distinctive methodological approach by which to study the preconditions of and resistances to the emergence of new sociocultural entities that challenge the "national" as the privileged associational principle. To be sure, the potential emergence of cosmopolitan orientations should not be misconstrued as an end to national identity. Rather, it suggests a reflexive interrogation of the validity of a historically specific and thus malleable conceptualization of the national itself. From this point of view, globalization cannot be reduced to external relations between increasingly interconnected national societies but must be seen as a vehicle for transforming the inner grammar of cultural and political identities. In order to specify the distinctiveness of such processes of "globalization from within," a cosmopolitan perspective seeks to overcome the habit of theorizing globalization through an either/or logic that relies on oppositions between the "inside" and "outside" or the "exogenous" and "endogenous." The notion of cosmopolitanization implies an interactive relationship between the global and the local by highlighting the transformative emergence of new, denationalized social spaces and cultural imaginaries through their interaction.

Much of the debate on cosmopolitanism revolves around implicit or contested understandings of belonging. This is doubtless compounded by the vagueness of the concept of identity itself (Brubaker and Cooper 2000). For most social scientists, strong forms of belonging are predicated on a naturalized image of the nation, with manifestations such as communitarianism and ethno-nationalism, to name two possibilities. Cosmopolitanism, by contrast, is often characterized (both in its normative version and by its nationalist opposition) as the breakdown of boundaries, referring to humans rather than embedded people. Underlying this dualistic perception is the assumption that belonging operates primarily (or sometimes even exclusively) in the context of communal allegiance expressive of thick solidarities. Conversely, Craig Calhoun reminds us that we need not succumb to the opposite fallacy, which presents cosmopolitan identity "as freedom from social belonging rather than a special form of belonging, a view from nowhere or everywhere, rather than from particular social spaces" (2003, 532). Our notion of cosmopolitanism not only demands a universalistic minimum but also presupposes a particularistic one that recognizes the existence of communal fate and attachment. The respective balance of particularism and universal modes, we suggest, can be identified in changing forms of memories and sovereignty.

In both national and cosmopolitan cases, the success of identification with distant others is ultimately predicated on a balanced notion of thick attachments with concrete others (e.g., kin, local) and thinner versions of solidarity (e.g., the nation, the global). The point is not that we dispense with thick forms of belonging, but rather that we explore identities as the coexistence of thick attachments and thin orientations. This view is premised on the notion that meaningful identities are predicated on particular attachments, as our identity is always embedded in the story of the communities from which we construct our identities. Particularism becomes a prerequisite for a cosmopolitan orientation. Rather than treat cosmopolitanism as negating nationalism, we see national attachments as potential mediators between the individual and the global horizons against which identifications unfold. Particular identities are thus not an obstruction to cosmopolitan identities but in many ways they are mutually constitutive.

In sum, a cosmopolitan perspective does not entail a denial of the persistent reality of the nation for social actors. It suggests, rather, that the contemporary nation-state itself and new forms of nationalism are best understood if the social-scientific observer adopts a cosmopolitan perspective. In this light, a cosmopolitan methodological shift derives its analytical force from elucidating the relationship between processes of actual cosmopolitanization and the persistence or resurgence of political self-descriptions that are tied to a nationalist normativity. Studying cosmopolitanized memories provides a diagnostic prism that allows us to historicize the balance of particular and universal perceptions rather than stipulate their mutual exclusiveness or a universal trajectory. These developments are not merely epiphenomenal but are integral to how memories of human rights operate. Accordingly, we attempt to highlight two dimensions of memory politics that strike us as particularly

important for theorizing the prominence of human rights and the transformation of sovereignty, and by extension the interactive relationship
of universal orientations and particular attachments. These are the fragmentation of memories and their decontextualization that facilitates the
abstraction of concrete historical suffering.

That memories are no longer beholden exclusively to the idea of the
nation-state is of central importance. Today there is a pervasive trend
toward national and global introspection that has prompted numerous
countries around the world to come to terms with their past (Levy and
Sznaider 2005). "Inventions of nationhood" during the nineteenth century were based on heroic conceptions and formative myths transmitted
by "traditional" and "exemplary" forms of narrativity. In contrast, the history of western European nation-states during the last quarter of the twentieth century was characterized by a self-critical narrative of their national
pasts. While traditional and exemplary narratives deploy historical events
to promote foundational myths, skeptical narratives also incorporate
events that focus on past injustices committed by one's own nation.

Given the centrality of western Europe for the articulation and dissemination of human rights discourse, a closer look at how memories of
human rights abuses are articulated in the context of Europeanization is
instructive. Despite its declarative commitments to openness and diversity, underneath much European cosmopolitanism remains a thick veneer
of European particularism masquerading as universalism. As such,
this universalism adheres to a long tradition of cosmopolitan thought
in Europe that goes back to Kant (1795/1991) and other Enlightenment
thinkers, one that attracted renewed ideological and political attention in
the aftermath of World War II. It is a tradition marked by a strong sense
of universal mission that emanated from the center of Europe and flowed
outward. Europeanism here essentially refers to a western European
model that took shape during the first postwar decade in the context of
Franco-German reconciliation and joint economic projects, and against
the backdrop of the emerging cold war. Nevertheless, Europe is in many
ways a captive of its own cosmopolitan human rights rhetoric.

Its shortcomings notwithstanding, the European case is paradigmatic,
as it serves as both an empirical and an analytical laboratory: empirically,

its policies of integration and the resulting demographic diversification facilitate and necessitate the formation of new forms of belonging; consequently, these changes pose the kind of analytical challenges for which methodological nationalism is no longer equipped. Lastly, the European case has modular functions beyond its borders, if only because of its political and economic centrality in the global age.

Lately this cosmopolitan trend has developed beyond western Europe—for instance, to former Communist countries that investigate their "sinful" past. But it does not stop there. For many, the model has been South Africa's Truth and Reconciliation Commission. This reckoning with the past and the accompanying "politics of regret" (Olick 2007) is an internal affair, but it is steered and fueled by external acts and attitudes. The proliferation of historical commissions and the active role of human rights organizations in public debates about usable pasts are but one example of this trend (Barkan and Karn 2006). What were once considered "normal" practices of nation building and routines of power, even when based on violence and warlike conduct, are now being reconceptualized as illegitimate human rights violations, for example, so-called ethnic cleansing (Diner 2007; Minow 1998). This is especially true for countries in central and eastern Europe whose borders were delineated on the principle of ethnic homogeneity after World War II, having failed to homogenize after World War I. Memories of ethnic assimilation and dissimilation are historically inscribed in the European experience. The key interpretive issue here is the transition from heroic nation-states to a form of statehood that establishes internal and external legitimacy through its support for skeptical narratives. Cosmopolitanized memories thus evolve in the context of remembered continuities that view the past of the nation through its willingness to come to terms with injustices committed in its name. The "normal" has turned into a crime, while at the same time criminals responsible for mass murder or genocide are turned into "normal" human beings.[6]

This focus on memories of past injustices is accompanied by another tendency, namely, the transition from *history politics*, which is characterized by a state-centric dynamic (through official commemorations, textbooks, etc.), to *memory history*, which corresponds to the fragmentation of memory and its privatization.[7] This transformation manifests itself in the changing relationship between memory and history. The difference between memory history and conventional historical narratives is instructive. History is a particularized idea of temporal sequences articulating some form of (national) development. Memory, on the other hand, represents a coexistence of simultaneous phenomena and a multitude of pasts. (National) history politics corresponds to the *telos* of modernity (as a kind of secularized, or civic, religion). Memory can dissolve this sequence, which is a constitutive part of history. Memory history is a particular mnemonic mode that moves away from state-supported (and state-supporting) national history.

The state's previous (attempted) monopoly on shaping collective pasts has given way to a fragmentation of memories borne by private, individual, scientific, ethnic, religious, and other mnemonic agents. Although the state continues to play an important role in how we remember its history, it now shares the field of meaning production with a host of other players. Modes of collective memory are being cosmopolitanized and also exist on supra- and subnational levels. The formation of cosmopolitan human rights memories does not eliminate the national perspective, but it makes nationhood one of several options of collective identification. As the state loses its privileged command over the production of collective values (e.g., nationalism), human rights memories become politically and culturally more consequential.

In both the national and the global cases, the success of identification with distant others is predicated on two conditions: (1) a changed notion from thick attachments with concrete others (kin, tribal) to thinner versions of solidarity with the nation and its symbolic personifications, and (2) the ability to produce shared memories that at once generate concrete references to heroic deeds of the nation or particular human rights atrocities and make it possible to draw abstract identifications from them (i.e., the need to forget the misdeeds of the nation, as Ernest Renan put it in 1882, and remember selectively, as the uneven pursuit of human rights appears to indicate).

The claim that the nation-state is an unproblematic container for solidarity is profoundly ahistorical. Ironically, when national cultures were invented, they were open to the same criticisms as those directed at global culture today. They were dismissed as superficial and inauthentic substitutes for local cultures that were once rich in tradition, and they were taken to task for being much too large and alienating. Surely, it was argued, nobody would ever identify with the impersonal image of the nation. As history has shown, this prediction was wrong. In his seminal 1983 treatise on the origins of nationalism, Benedict Anderson quips about the limits of solidarity when he poses the rhetorical question "Who would be willing to die for the European Community?" This comes as something of a surprise, given Anderson's constructivist approach, which stipulates that all communities, and especially nations, are entities that are fundamentally imagined. The very belief that there is something fundamental at their root is the result of a conscious myth-building process. To come into existence, the nation-state at the *fin de siècle* depended on a process by which existing societies used representations to turn themselves into new wholes that would act immediately on people's feelings and on which they could base their identities—in short, making them into groups with which individuals could identify. The essential point of Anderson's thesis, which is often overlooked, is that a new system of values requiring self-sacrifice and willingness to live together is necessary in the transition to nationhood. In the premodern era, solidarity was based primarily on direct contact with the "Other" (ethical boundaries corresponded to village boundaries); with the "nationalization of the masses," it became necessary to identify with many other people via an "imagined community" whom one could not possibly get to know personally. We do not know each other, and yet we feel united as citizens of the same country.

This nation-building process, we suggest, parallels the course of globalization at the beginning of the twenty-first century. The ability of representations to give a sense to life is not ontologically but sociologically determined. If the nation is the basis for authentic feelings and collective memory, as the critics of global culture seem almost unanimous in maintaining, then it cannot be argued that representations are a superficial substitute for authentic experience. The nation is literally inconceivable without an imagined community (Anderson 1983). Representations are the basis of this authenticity, and there is nothing theoretically or empirically inconceivable about their providing such a basis on a global level.

The salience of universal (human) or particular (national) rights is mediated by, among other things, the extent to which memories of past human rights abuses are transmitted as concrete or abstract forms, the latter proliferating with the cosmopolitanization of memories. Human rights matter only to the extent that their universality is recognized. This recognition, in turn, is predicated on a process of decontextualization by which memories of concrete (particular) atrocities are transformed into abstract (universal) violations of humanity. Without this decontextualization it is difficult to recontextualize memories of human rights as abstract categories and thus ensure their recognition as universal lessons for humanity.

Moreover, this process of abstraction does little to change the fact that communities transmit different memories of the past, based largely on the extent to which memories of past abuses are a concrete part of shared experiences or whether they lack the kind of proximity or distance that allows them to become abstract principles. Accordingly, the strength of human rights principles in a given national context is the product of the tenuous balance between particular (concrete) and universal (decontextualized) memories. The latter are in essence a form of forgetting. The relationship between memory and forgetting has received significant attention in the literature (Ricoeur 1999). Contrary to most views, however, we do not treat memory as an antidote to forgetting. Instead we suggest that institutionalized memories of human rights abuses inexorably imply forgetting. The institutionalization of such memories, and thus their ability to mobilize legitimate political claims, is based largely on the process of decontextualization, which in turn requires a shift from concrete memories to abstract remembrance. In other words, there is a move away from the concrete (i.e., particular) experience toward a more abstract (i.e., universal) message. Consequently, we are witness to a shift consisting of the institutionalization of the remembrance of barbarous acts at the expense of memories of the barbarity of these acts.

The distinction between memory and remembrance is not incidental. Nor can it be reduced to the so-called instrumentalization of memories.

Memory vacillating between the concrete and the abstract, and its implied decontextualization, can be related to three dimensions. It inheres in the course of action that gives memories their ritualistic strength. Ritualization depends on mediation, which by definition requires a certain form of abstraction. Considering the various channels through which memories of past human rights abuses are communicated, we consider this a process of mediated forgetting. Failure to remember is also implied insofar as proximity to that which is remembered can shape the relative political-cultural significance it has for a community. Put differently, the universality of human rights necessitates a certain distance from the actual events that are being remembered. Lastly, the immanence of this dynamic is not just the product of historical and geographic proximity; it is also the result of temporal distance from the events that are being remembered.

This temporal distance is captured in Jan Assmann's distinction between communicative and cultural memory. Communicative memory refers to memories based on group-specific carriers and is expressed through the daily encounters and stories of people involved in the events that are being remembered. Cultural memory exists independent of its carriers and is reproduced through media and commemorative institutions. "What is at stake is the transformation of communicative, i.e., lived and witness-embodied, memory into cultural, i.e., institutionally shaped and sustained, memory, that is, into a 'cultural mnemotechnique'" (Assmann 1991, 343). This transition corresponds to our argument about the inevitable shift from the concrete to the abstract. Cultural memory turns history into narrative and shifts attention from fact-driven, i.e., particular history, to remembered history, i.e., produced through ritualization and other forms of representation.

One way of looking at this phenomenon empirically is to focus on the decontextualization of memories of human rights abuses, which functions as a prerequisite for the spread of human rights as a universally recognized idiom. The decontextualization of particular memories of human rights abuses and their universal reappropriation can be addressed by distinguishing between who is remembering and what is remembered. Moreover, cosmopolitan memories of human rights abuses are circumscribed by the historical occurrence of a forgiveness narrative that has further contributed to the shift from memory to remembrance and a corresponding transition from concrete individual to more abstract collective dimensions. Memories of human rights violations have become a subject of public negotiations and have been subjected to the imperatives of forgiveness and reconciliation (Levy and Sznaider 2006a).

By historicizing human rights, we propose a political sociology of human rights that is not based on some universalized metaphysical appeal but is transmitted primarily through the proliferation of globally produced memories of failures to address human rights abuses. These mnemonic practices are firmly embodied in historical references and institutional manifestations. The main difference between the universalist origins of human rights and their recent cosmopolitan manifestations is that the latter unfold against the background of a globalized imagination. This does not imply convergence or homogenization but rather the emergence of a locally situated recognition that sees humanity as a meaningful category of membership, not in a normative but in a political, cultural, and legally consequential terminology that is in line with denationalized conceptions of membership. Exclusion from the nation is no longer synonymous with exclusion from the protection of the state. The continuous transposition of cosmopolitan memories about failures to prevent human rights abuses has changed the conditions of membership. The surplus of legitimacy that human rights conceptions currently enjoy is neither irreversible nor evenly distributed. This should not be a reason for despair but rather the starting point for a continuous reflexive engagement with and refinement of a theory of human rights.

This book is intended to contribute to this effort by addressing the significance of human rights principles for both social and political theory and the shadow cast by historical memories over domestic and international politics. Given the national assumptions that inform most conceptualizations of (citizenship) rights, a theory of rights beyond the national frame has yet to be constructed. As we show in the next chapter, the aforementioned developments have spurred renewed attention to theories of rights. The contingent circumstances under which human rights affect state sovereignty also have immediate bearing on our ability to theorize about human rights. Previously trapped in a national cage, the epistemological context for advancing a social theory of human rights is now more favorable. This is not necessarily a function of the salience of the human rights regime itself, which is rather fragile, but is primarily the result of the decoupling of nation and state that both reflects and contributes to a nation-transcending conception of membership and solidarity. Globalization has propelled the ascendance of cosmopolitan norms embodied in the human rights regime and challenges the nation-centric foundations of sociology. The impact of memories of human rights failures on the transformation of sovereignty has not led to the erosion of the state. On the contrary, the human rights orientation has become a necessary condition for maintaining state legitimacy.

From a theoretical vantage point, this provides a formidable opportunity to move beyond the old dichotomy of universalism and particularism and the nation-centric focus, which has long been a major impediment to a sociology of human rights. A large part of the problem for social scientists is the quagmire of universalism and particularism, as they fear universal claims and are bound to claims of culture, nations, and classes. The opposition of the executive board of the American Anthropological Association (AAA) to the drafting of the Universal Declaration of Human Rights in 1947 (American Anthropological Association 1947) was typical. The 1947 statement apparently caused much embarrassment to the association and its members and was amended—some forty years later (see Engle 2001)—thus highlighting its inability to escape the power of the human rights regime. Anthropologists, like other social scientists, recognize the normative power of human rights. In 1999 they declared their clear commitment to them while trying to preserve the notion of collective rights so dear to social scientists (see also Goodale 2007). The changing stance of the AAA captures the general dilemma social scientists must confront when dealing with human rights as a system of moral ideals—namely, how cultural pluralism and human diversity coupled with respect for culture can be combined with a commitment to norms and ideals binding for all mankind.

The AAA did indeed believe that human rights are a form of Western or colonial imposition on other cultures. This is why it affirmed that "respect for differences between cultures is validated by the scientific fact that no technique of qualitatively evaluating cultures has been discovered" (AAA 1947, 542). Furthermore, "standards and values are relative to the culture from which they derive so that any attempt to formulate postulates that grow out of the beliefs or moral codes of one culture must to that extent detract from the applicability of any Declaration of Human Rights to mankind as a whole" (543). The AAA thus set the stage for the social-scientific community to look at human rights in terms of imposition and cultural arrogance. As anthropologists, they advocated cultural relativism over universalism. In many ways the human rights debate is still caught between these two poles. Is there a way out of the quagmire between universal ideals, as expressed in human rights, and respect for particularity, which often may serve as a cover for authorizing atrocities with impunity? The concept of cosmopolitanism can act as a linking mechanism between universalism and particularism that could lead to a better sociological grasp of human rights. In chapters 2 and 3 we develop the theoretical issues articulating a sociology of human rights and related conceptualizations of sovereignty.

Chapters 4 through 7 provide a historical sociology of how memories of past injustices crystallized into a human rights regime. Methodologically, we engage in a two-pronged approach. We look at the institutional developments but do so with a particular focus on memory. Both salience and malleability of memory are best assessed with a mnemo-historical approach. According to Jan Assmann (1997), mnemo-history is not about the exploration of the past per se but rather is concerned with how a particular past is remembered. Here the past is not merely subject to the kind of presentist instrumentalism where historical pasts serve the expediencies of the politics *du jour;* the past as such is invented, shaped, and reconstructed by the present. How histories are remembered and by extension distorted over time emerges as the main focus of our analytic pursuits. What matters here is not so much the factuality of these memories but their actuality.

We pay particular attention to how memories suffuse legal proceedings, especially trials that address human rights abuses. The transformative power of cosmopolitanized memories, we argue, is evidenced in the juridification of politics. The political will of states to engage legally with memories of rights abuses is becoming a central factor for their legitimate standing in the international community and increasingly also a domestic source of legitimacy. We treat law, therefore, as a medium of collective memory. Certainly legal traditions remain bound to national traditions, but even these national traditions have to take into account and heed transnational rules and regulations. Recent studies in the sociology of law have pointed to the fact that trials and other legal procedures institutionalize remembering and forgetting (Booth 2006; Misztal 2001; Osiel 1997; Savelsberg and King 2007). On the other hand, trials have to proclaim truth and justice, which often do not correspond to memory. Constructions of what can be called "legal memory" try to balance these apparently contradictory aspirations. Indeed, many of these legal premises are reenacted through the mnemonic dimensions of court trials.

Our analysis shows how recent trials related to human rights abuses are an important locus for the production of cosmopolitan ideals and their criticism, especially when considering the strong legal dimensions of contemporary global politics. We treat this development not merely as a legal process but as a socially embedded, meaning-producing act. Trials are transformative opportunities, where memories of grave injustices are addressed in rituals of restitution and renewal (Osiel 1997). Justice itself becomes a form of remembrance. With the consolidation of the human rights regime, however, these memories are no longer coextensive with the nation-state but revolve around the contested boundaries of particular and universal identifications.   *Or not ...*

War crime trials in particular do not merely edify histories; they also function as a remedy for amnesia (Douglas 2001). Beyond the potential of trials to create legal precedents, because of their public dramaturgy they also attract widespread media attention. Their dramatic enactment ensures that war crime trials not only change the law from within but enjoy ritualized attention, thus serving broader educational and moral purposes. Three didactic dimensions characterize the relationship of law and memory as evidenced in war crime trials. One relates to legitimacy, in the sense that legality itself is restored after its suspension through crimes against humanity. The second is the moral pedagogy that underlies these trials. Third, through the category of crimes against humanity, questions of inclusion and exclusion as well as the legal limits of the nation-state are renegotiated (Pendas 2002). Trials are thus moments of transformative opportunity for cosmopolitanization. As could clearly be observed in the former Yugoslavia, in Rwanda, and even in Iraq, war crime trials function as hybrid legal zones where the boundaries of particular identities and universal orientations are negotiated. Our historical analysis pays particular attention to post–World War II war crime trials and their political-cultural significance for the iconization of the Holocaust, and, by extension, the ways in which memories of past human rights abuses have become a prominent feature of international law.

The intersection of law and memory is not limited to the ritualistic dimension of war crime trials, because "judicial memories" are also evidenced in the transformation of international law itself (Dezalay and Garth 2006). A key moment of the cosmopolitanization of sovereignty resides in the juridification of global politics. Cosmopolitan legality can assume the power of nation-transcending legitimacy. Since the 1990s international law has been recast as an alternative discourse "framed in the universalizing language of human rights. . . . The new paradigm weds traditional humanitarianism with the law of human rights, causing a shift away from states as the dominant subjects of International Law to include 'persons' and 'peoples.' . . . The emerging legal regimes play a role in shaping current political policymaking, chiefly by reframing and restructuring the discourse in international affairs in a legalist direction" (Teitel 2003, 362–66).

The prominence of international law itself is not new and enjoyed widespread support in the "international" period during the nineteenth century. "However, what is new is the notion that law itself can define what constitutes peace and stability internationally, and further that it could somehow displace politics to resolve international conflict" (ibid., 385). This juridification of political relations is a central feature in the institutionalization of the human rights regime, and it is sustained, among other things, by self-conscious references to memories of past abuses. At the same time, the legal role of memory and the legal construction of memory are constrained. We are bound by our traditions when we change them. Hence it is crucial to examine these traditions. The legal examples presented in the following chapters convey both the constructivist dimension of rights talk and the path-dependency of cosmopolitanized memories.

While independence and self-determination remain potent principles in world affairs, symbolic-political appeals for national rights are increasingly gauged by how they are related to the legal recognition of human rights and thus reconfigure the nation-state model. To be sure, we are not positing the end of the national, but rather its diminishing normative return. We recognize that cosmopolitanization can incur renationalization—but in a form very different from traditional nationalism.[8] The latter was the main legitimating principle in the first half of the twentieth century and was state sponsored. Now it presents itself defensively and frequently does not emanate from the state. Consequently, in establishing a new conceptual framework, we are primarily arguing for a methodological gestalt switch. New forms of retribalization can no longer be understood through older models of nationhood but rather against an emerging world-cultural principle of cosmopolitanism that finds it foremost expression in the institutionalization of the human rights regime.

In deploying this cosmopolitan methodology and stressing memory practices, we approach the notion of an international convergence of rights policies and universalization with some reservations. It is important to distinguish contemporary cosmopolitan manifestations from the strong international impulses that contributed to the original institutional manifestations of human rights at the end of the nineteenth century. Lasting until the beginning of World War II, this period witnessed significant growth in international organizations and laws dedicated to human rights. This internationalist era was primarily geared toward the consolidation of nation-state sovereignty. In contrast, the cosmopolitanization of the past two decades is indicative of a recasting of the state-society-nation relationship. While the "old internationalism" regulated the relations between nation-states and sanctified their particularism, the "new cosmopolitanism" challenges the primacy of the nation and emphasizes the cosmopolitan foundations of global interdependencies. Our cosmopolitan approach thus serves as a corrective to expectations of convergence. Structural similarities do not necessarily determine the meanings attached to human rights norms in particular national contexts.

Memories of human rights abuses, as well as failures to address them in time, are thus facets of a conflictual conception of collective memory. We illustrate this dynamic in chapter 8, via a discussion of authors who refuse to accept the implied connection between memory and forgiveness and instead articulate a space in which resentment becomes part of the human rights equation. That the integrative role of memory operates through self-conscious engagement with conflict is also evidenced in chapter 9, which examines the competing memories of human rights abuses as they prevail in western and eastern-central Europe. Memory is diverse and plural. It tells more than one story. Often these stories are contradictory and do not recount one single narrative. And they do not need to. Witnesses in trials make this point quite clearly. This is particularly relevant to contemporary debates in liberal democracies where national cultures and their homogeneous conceptions of the collectivity are challenged by the multicultural composition of their societies.

We conclude the book with a discussion of the salience and limits of the human rights regime in the context of global terrorism, now symbolized by the iconic 9/11. Global terrorism has prodded renewed discussions about the relationship of human rights and sovereign prerogatives. Rather than view them as mutually exclusive, we discuss how that relationship is changing in a global context and how the link remains closely tied to specific experiences. Here, too, cosmopolitan memories coexist with memories of communal loss and trauma. Reactions against the very universality of human rights have become an important feature of how particular identities are negotiated. Thus, rather than treat national sentiments and other expressions of particular identification as anachronistic, we show how they are being addressed in a new context of global interdependency and related "clashes of memories." Collectivities remember their vulnerabilities in different ways, diachronically but also cross-culturally. In light of such dis-simultaneities, antagonisms persist and, depending on the salience of actual threats and fears, cannot be reconciled by simple recourse to instrumental rationality or universality. In short, a plurality of memories about human frailty and accompanying rights help constitute the political and cultural salience of human rights. A theory of human rights must reckon with these plural and sometimes fragmented memories. Such a theory is not only about convergence and universalism but is also about differences expressed in communal memories and continuing antagonisms. In contrast to the first half of the twentieth century and until the dissolution of the bipolar world, however, these tensions and the accompanying clashes of memories now unfold against the backdrop of a cosmopolitan ideal that, although mostly found in Europe, has become a global norm against which particularism is articulated.

The significance of the human rights regime thus goes beyond the prevention of gross injustices. It could even be argued that the preventive apparatus is one of the least successful aspects of this regime. But the human rights regime also recasts the national premises of solidarity, which are no longer based on homogeneity but rather on the acceptance of difference. This is not a normative pledge for another version of "unity in diversity" but a development that raises questions about the unifying potential associated with human rights norms and the power of the human rights regime to inculcate values of solidarity that transcend national, tribal, or ethnic ties (Flynn 2009). This cosmopolitanization is not some utopia of tolerance but implies that particular group identifications have a relational rather than a categorical quality (Brubaker 2002). Groups do remember their own past. This is a given. But this "own past" and often the grievances that come with that past are now frequently set in relation and with reference to the legitimating purchase of cosmopolitan values and attendant ideals of human rights.

SOCIOLOGY AND HUMAN RIGHTS

Despite the prominence of human rights in the realm of social movement activism and the incorporation of legal mechanisms into highly institutionalized regimes, the subject of human rights remains a theoretical laggard in the sociological field (Turner 2006). To be sure, there are numerous important empirical works that stress the global ascendance of a human rights regime as an antidote to powerful organizations (Sjoberg, Gill, and Williams 2001). The emergence of NGOs, INGOs (international nongovernmental organizations), and social movements challenging the legitimacy of nation-states that violate human rights is also well documented (Boli and Thomas 1999; Wotipka and Tsutsui 2008). In spite of successful efforts started as late as 2007 to add a human rights section to the official registry of the American Sociological Association, sociologists have hardly developed a theory of human rights (Turner 1995; Somers and Roberts 2008).

A brief and necessarily schematic overview of the causes of this lacuna is instructive. Given the origins of the field of sociology, this conceptual oversight is not accidental but in fact is closely related to the nation-centric foundations of sociology and the concomitant tensions between particularism and universalism. A sociology of human rights may appear to be a contradiction in terms. Sociology is about social groups, particular experiences, and how people, embedded in space and time, make sense of their lives and give meaning to their world. It deals with power and interests and the social bases of our experiences. Human rights, by contrast, are about human beings in general, irrespective of temporal or spatial references, not about territorially confined groups and their frontiers. Human rights are inviolable and apply to humanity as a whole and they are about dignity. Rights and dignity go together, and they need no sociological garb.

In the history of political thought, this point is captured in conceptual differences drawn between Immanuel Kant and Jean-Jacques Rousseau. Kant's influence (see especially his view of universality and the categorical imperative as developed in his *Groundwork for the Metaphysics of Morals* [1785]) on current human rights discourse has been decisive. Notions of equal moral worth, universalism, individualism, autonomy, and self-determination still provide the rational universal foundation for human rights beyond communal attachments and political expediency. Sociology emerged from criticism of exactly this kind of Enlightenment universalism, which forms the normative basis of much current thinking about human rights. A universal human rights regime is not the "general will" of modern democracy, as mapped by Rousseau onto the nation and woven into the sociological theories of Durkheim and Weber. Rousseau's "general will" is not only the foundation of modern relativism; it is also the source of the modern idea of the nation not merely as a collection of followers but as the institution that reconciles freedom and determinism. Rousseau heralded the birth of society as national society. Over the course of the twentieth century, the "general" in his "general will" became synonymous with the universal, and this universal is largely considered to be the nation. The close association of citizenship with the nation-state leaves little conceptual space for a universal articulation of rights. Rights are now understood as citizenship rights and are relevant for citizens, not universal men. This is how methodological nationalism and universalism are linked in sociological theory. Thus the dearth of social theorizing on human rights is primarily the result of the nation-building project that coincided with the birth of sociology and remains the hallmark of social theory. This national focus is compounded by the Hobbesian social contract between a collectivity and a sovereign. Since the protection of a particular community has primacy, there is little conceptual and political space left for a nation-transcending approach. Trapped in a national container, the broader sociological enterprise revolves around mechanisms of exclusion and inclusion, which is about social groups and solidarity. The nation is the most prominent category, with manifestations such as communitarianism and ethnonationalism at opposite ends of the scale. By contrast, human rights are about the breakdown of boundaries, and about humans rather than embedded people, suggesting thin identifications that are not based on communal allegiance or thick solidarities.

Moreover, sociological thinking counters the belief that politics should be guided by theoretical doctrine, universal principles, and appeals to abstract rights. The professionalization of sociology is predicated on positivism and empiricism in contradistinction to the normativity of philosophical concepts. As Somers and Roberts point out, "A division of labor and turf instead divides sociologists who write about people who fight for rights from philosophers who worry about the meaning and justification of those rights. To be sure, there are those who instrumentalize rights as the 'masks of true interests' or as market-driven utilities—thus demonstrating their affinity for the categories of preferences or interests. Yet this empirical reduction depletes rights of their normativity, bypassing the implications of their widespread violation and/or the justificatory exigencies of establishing them in the first place" (2008, 4).

The idea that sociology is about material and ideal interests, whereas human rights are universal and devoid of particular interests, remains a central organizing wedge for disciplinary divisions. This disparity is also frequently invoked when sociologists seek to debunk the universality of human rights by referring to them as a new form of imperialism and a threat to particular cultural values (Evans 2001; Waters 1996), essentially confirming the material bias of sociological analysis. But it is precisely the kind of metaphysical zeal sociological thinking rejects that is at the heart of the contemporary project for a global human rights regime. Human rights have turned into issues of belief and carry an aura of the sacred (Ignatieff 2004). In a strong view of cultural sociology, the strength of human rights norms cannot be reduced to instrumental or coercive factors. Rather, the cultural salience of human rights norms "is embedded to some extent in a horizon of affect and meaning. This internal environment is one toward which the actor can never be fully instrumental or reflexive. It is, rather, an ideal resource that partially enables and partially constrains action. . . . Similarly, a belief in the possibility of a cultural sociology implies that institutions, no matter how impersonal or technocratic, have an ideal foundation that fundamentally shapes their organization and goals and provides the structured context for debates over their legitimation" (Alexander 2003, 12). It is, therefore, a challenge to formulate a sociological analysis of human rights that accounts for but does not reduce them to power struggles or the politics of material interests.

By excluding the universality of human rights, sociology has relegated their foundational assumptions to the realm of normative philosophical analysis. But there need be no dichotomy between social constructionist and foundational accounts of human rights. As Turner put it, "it is perfectly consistent to argue that human rights can have a foundationalist ontology in the notion that human beings are frail and accept the argument that human rights will be constructed in a contingent and variable way according to the specific characteristics of the societies in which they are developed and a particular outcome of political struggles over interests" (1997, 566). Furthermore, this foundational fallacy "presents a problem for sociology, in which cultural relativism and the fact-value distinction have largely destroyed the classical tradition of the natural-law basis for rights discourse" (Turner 1993, 489). Sociology is about causality and historicism. Natural law takes the opposite tack, in that it claims that there is a firm foundation in nature for rights and that they are not subject to choice (Strauss 1955). Consequently, the prevalence of the national and its methodological penchant in the social sciences have until recently impeded the development of a systematic body of theoretical thought on human rights.

TOWARD A SOCIOLOGY OF HUMAN RIGHTS

To overcome some of these obstacles to the theorizing of a sociology of rights, we suggest a historical approach based on a dual strategy that recognizes the contingency of foundational assumptions as well as the malleability of ontological principles. Since globalization challenges these national presuppositions, human rights have become a relevant political and normative category. We are thus at a historical juncture where there is an opportunity to advance a theory of human rights. Arguably this task can be addressed in purely conceptual terms. The conditions for theorizing rights are contingent on historical events (and analysis) that account for the salience of a particular rights discourse and the associated power of language, and the symbolism attributed to human life (Connell 1995). Translated into social theory, this entails our recognition that human rights have assumed a sacred status (Hopgood 2009), an association that was very much part of the spirit of the Universal Declaration of Human Rights. As René Cassin, who co-drafted the declaration, for which he received the Nobel Peace Prize in 1968, noted, "the expression: God created Man in his own Image characterizes both that *prise de conscience* and the religious form which it adopted initially. Secularization followed. The dignity of man has been reaffirmed by philosophers, sociologists, and statesmen regardless of religious beliefs, and has been detached from religious credos or cults. What is incontestable is the permanence of the idea through the centuries and despite the most profound divergences of interpretation of the doctrine" (1971, 14).

Thus a sociology of human rights is not a contradiction in terms but in many ways is akin to a sociology of religion in which one explores the "functions" of rights and looks at the transcendental moments of our existence, as in Durkheim's foundational *Elementary Forms of Religious Life* (1912). For Durkheim, moral ideas reflect social boundaries that are at their broadest in a democracy. The greater mutual interdependency brought about through an elaborate division of labor enables the moral sense to expand and become more abstract and universal. Durkheim's utopian goal was to create a secular rational ethic. Collective memories, in his view, were the remnants of a corporate and divided society. The challenge has always been to turn his sociological insights into a contemporary framework (for good examples, see Boltanski 1999; Silverstone 2007; Sznaider 2001). Unlike philosophical debates about the nature of morality, however, Durkheim's sociology of morals starts from moral facts, not from moral obligations: "There is between men an internal bond, which manifests itself in affections, sympathy, language, civil society, and is yet something more profound than all that, hidden in the recesses of the human essence. . . . Men, bound by a community of essence cannot say 'I am indifferent to what concerns others.' But whatever this solidarity may be, whatever its nature and its origins, it can only be presented as a fact, with no basis for presenting it as a duty" (Durkheim 1997, 413–14).

This passage is from the preface to the first edition of the *Division of Labor*. It constitutes an argument against Kantian and utilitarian ideas of morality and presents an outline for an empirical sociology of moral values. Durkheim was primarily interested in what held people together in an age of individualism. His answer was that the "division of labor" is not only a law of history but also the sole basis for ethical and social life. Durkheim claimed that moral rules are only moral in relation to certain social and historical conditions. Since the division of labor is the chief source of social solidarity, it correlatively becomes the foundation of moral order. This, of course, defines Durkheim as a moral relativist, but whereas in philosophy, theories of moral obligation do not depend on consensus, in sociology they do. With his empirical sociology of morals, Durkheim attempted to avoid both under- and oversocialized conceptions of humanity, thus taking both agency and social determinism into account. Durkheim carved out a sociological position in his opposition to philosophical views of ethics, whether Kantian or utilitarian. This is what we seek to accomplish in our analysis of the impact of memories on human rights consciousness and politics.

In contrast to the Kantian tradition, Durkheim believed that justice in a modern democratic society begins with our emotional engagement in the world. We do not only "think" the world but "feel" it, especially when it comes to pain and pleasure. Given that the joy of benevolence is the basis of moral sentiments, Durkheim concurred with the rational philosophers that cruelty and suffering are out of place in an ordered universe. In his sociology of morals, rationalism and utilitarianism are interwoven. Durkheim showed that both duty and the pursuit of the "good" are products of social interaction in specific social and historical circumstances. His theory was an attempt to restore the moral dimension of sociology by referring to eighteenth-century formulations of natural sympathy and compassion (for an analysis of Durkheim as a precursor to current cosmopolitan sensibilities, see Turner 2006). Social facts evolve out of moral facts. His concept of memory was also shaped by the events of World War I and the constant tensions between patriotism and "world patriotism" (or between the polis and the cosmos). Durkheim saw no contradiction between these two sentiments as long as they fostered a just and rational world. His position contains a clear condemnation of contemporary criticism of human rights politics that perceives this form of politics as merely serving the narrow interests of specific groups.

Clearly, accepting this view as a presupposition alone does not relieve us of the leap of faith we must make when "believing" in the validity of human rights, but this defense is not much different from, say, the still pervasive implied validation of reason and rationality, postmodernism notwithstanding. By historicizing human rights, we show that the "dignity of man" is not an eternal truth but a construct with strong social underpinnings. One cannot take as a given that what we call "human rights violations" today also moved people to take action in other eras. Rather, we examine how human rights norms have become a politically and culturally meaningful language with strong institutional manifestations.

GLOBALLY MEDIA(TED) HUMAN RIGHTS AND COMPASSION

There has been a change in moral sentiments since 1945. Memories of the great wars have transformed human rights sensibilities, at least in Western liberal democracies. These new sensibilities have become a major factor when it comes to understanding human rights. Today, more than sixty years after the end of the war, it is almost impossible to watch the news on TV or surf the Internet without encountering blatant violations of the rights of others. These others are complete strangers to the spectators who are constantly forced to somehow integrate their sufferings into their daily lives. What should or can be done? And why care? Are we as spectators simply citizens of our own little "polis," or are we citizens of the "cosmos"? Can there be a cosmopolitan reaction to these spectacles? Are "we" responsible for the suffering of remote others? How should people respond when confronted with pictures of the beaten, tortured, and murdered? With compassion? What does compassion mean in the context of a globalized human rights politics? Compassion involves an active moral impetus to address others' suffering. Directed toward those outside the scope of personal knowledge, it becomes public compassion, shaping moral obligations to strangers in public arenas. This is the foundation for the recognition of human rights. Like human rights, compassion expresses a strong belief in universal benevolence, optimism, and the idea that happiness can be achieved in this life on earth.

There is a strong relationship between human rights consciousness and the emergence of a globalized cosmopolitan and liberal society, with its distinctive features of an expanded global awareness of the presence of others and the equal worth of human beings driven by memories of past human rights violations. Through these memories and their institutionalization in international conventions, the nature and sentiment of compassion have changed. Cruelty is now understood as the infliction of unwarranted suffering, and compassion is an organized, public response to this evil, as in human rights politics. With the lessening of profoundly categorical and corporate social distinctions triggered by the memories of barbarism, compassion can become more extensive and set a politics of human rights in motion. The capacity to identify with others, and in particular with others' pain, is promoted by the profound belief that others are similar to us. This identification is based on ontological equality.

Both the "memory imperative" and the recognition of the Other, however, require recurrent forms of mediation in order to sustain the human rights regime. Here the globalization of media images plays a crucial role (Tester 2001). Compassion enters into current debates on the universal and contextual foundations of ethics as depicted in the global media. Globalization transforms culture and the vocabulary used to produce meaning. This transformation becomes most evident when the particularities that make up a culture are divorced from their original spatial (i.e., local and national) contexts. Culture can no longer be understood as a closed national space, because it now competes constantly with other spaces. Transnational media and mass culture such as film and music loosen the national framework without abandoning it entirely. The globalization of communication technologies challenges national identities by confronting the viewer with the presence of others (Morley and Robins 1995). In the process, ideas about the world come into conflict with ideas about the nation. Even television viewers who never leave their hometown must integrate global value systems that are produced elsewhere into their national frame of reference. The rise of rapid, electronically based communication has led to an interlocked system without national borders. The immediate speed and imagery of the new global communications facilitate a shared consciousness and cosmopolitan memories that span territorial and linguistic borders.

Developments in the field of communications go hand in hand with new forms of memory. According to Hutton (1993), oral cultures rely on memories of lived experiences. In cultures of literacy, however, we "read" to retrieve forgotten wisdom from the past. The invention of the printing press to produce books and newspapers was crucial in this process of reconstructing the past. How do the new global media transform collective memory? The technological revolution that introduced the printing press textualized culture. The printed text led to an externalization of knowledge and laid the foundation for reference to shared knowledge. The global media have led to yet another revolution in the reception of knowledge, values, and memories by promoting a visual culture. We now remember things with the aid of images, which helps to explain why exhibitions, films, memorials, and other media are becoming so important.

Many of these global developments are possible only because of technological breakthroughs in electronic media. One feature that is particularly salient for the globalization of human rights discourse is the rise of media events, where a live and concentrated local action can be shared by the world. This is how the global is transported into the local. Distant others can be part of, and engender, the strong emotions of everyday life. According to Dayan and Katz (1992), media events are festivities that provide viewers with the opportunity to concentrate on shared principles and collective memory. They are characterized by the impression they give of being "live." Even when the focus is on conflicts, media events shape a common understanding of the event in so far as such events are often regarded as important dates that are meaningful to large groups of people. Through these events, news from the entire world enters local life. Not only is the local seen as part of a larger global context, but the world itself has a significance that has a political, cultural, and moral impact. Given the intensity and extensiveness of such media events, the globalized media play a major role in the propagation of a shared global moral universe based on human rather than national rights.

Even so, many scholars treat audiences as passive vessels subjected to dominant readings of media frames. For some of these critics, the media are only interested in human suffering inasmuch as it can be commodified. Human suffering here is just another lucrative product, since the media thrive on the sale of human tragedies (Moeller 1999). "Photojournalistic representations may frame human misery in ways that foster the detached or voyeuristic contemplation of alien experience. The objectification of suffering persons may either exploit misery or allow others to exploit it as consumers of tragedy who then reproduce pernicious contrasts between advanced social systems and hopelessly backward ways of life" (Linklater 2007, 28). For others, human rights discourse is presented as a justification for Western imperialist countries to extend their domination over the developing world (Žižek 2005; Chomsky 1999). Less a criticism of human rights themselves, they object to the politics conducted mainly in the form of intervention in other countries in the name of new-fashioned human rights rhetoric rather than old-fashioned power politics.

But isn't rhetoric worth something? We think it is and we show how human rights rhetoric can transform state sovereignty to a certain extent and mobilize people for political action. The motivations for this action can differ. "The question is whether the extension of human solidarity depends not only on emotional identification and compassion but also on feelings of guilt or shame when harm is caused or when little is done to alleviate misery. The conjecture is that shame and guilt along with compassion must become 'cosmopolitan emotions'" (Linklater 2007, 27). In other words, memories of past human rights abuses and failures to prevent them are an integral part of this dynamic. Even if the critics are convinced that the spectacle of distant suffering is devoid of moral consequences and selective, it does carry weight when it resonates with audiences' preconceived notions. This makes the wheels of human rights turn anew.

Another criticism of the media portrayal of human suffering is known as "compassion fatigue" (Sontag 2003). As Keith Tester notes, we are "becoming so used to the spectacle of dreadful events, misery or suffering that we stop noticing them. We are bored when we see one more tortured corpse on the television and we are left unmoved" (2001, 13). While it is perfectly reasonable to consider these negative features part of the global media, there is little question that a moral proposal is made to the viewer, one that can be accepted or rejected but can hardly be ignored. Even the viewer whose compassion for others is not triggered by stories and images of the suffering of distant others must come to terms with them. In global times the media are not only decisive in accelerating boundary-transcending processes; they constantly remind us that the stories we tell ourselves are not the only sources of identification.

Empirical studies of the human rights–media link indicate that media pervasiveness in the human rights discourse generates a greater resonance than one would expect from the kind of reductionist instrumentalism that permeates most skeptical approaches. Studying audience responses to human suffering, Birgitta Höijer's (2004) survey of people's reactions to images of violence suggests a more complex tale of global compassion. A little more than half of those surveyed (51 percent) responded that "they often or quite often do react to the pictures of distant suffering. About a quarter of the public (23 percent) said they were totally indifferent and do not react at all, and 14 percent said they react sometimes but very seldom. Some (7 percent) gave unclear answers that could not be categorized. . . . Women react with compassion more often than men, and elderly people much more often than younger people" (519). Compassion is further conditioned by the kind of visuals the audience is exposed to. Pictures of suffering of innocent civilians are more likely to elicit emotional reactions than similar pictures of soldiers. Who qualifies as a deserving victim is also a matter of dispute. But, as a general rule, "the audience accepts the dominant victim of the media and regards children, women and the elderly as ideal victims deserving compassion" (521). It should be noted that these results would probably be even more differentiated if the surveyed group of Swedes and Norwegians were replaced by, say, Kosovars, Israelis, Palestinians, Iraqis, or any other group of civilians whose memories of violence are of recent vintage or, worse, part of their everyday life.

However, our discussion of Höijer's study is not based merely on the empirical support it lends to global compassion; in addition, it reinforces our position that the human rights regime needs to be seen through a cosmopolitan lens. Rather than indulge in illusory universalism or succumb to the notion that the alleged omnipotence of the universal is nothing but a cover-up for Western domination, cosmopolitanization implies the erosion of distinct boundaries dividing markets, states, civilizations, cultures, and, not least, the lifeworlds of different peoples, and its consequences and the involuntary confrontation with the alien Other all over the globe. According to Beck (2001), this is a process of internal globalization and takes place in national and local lifeworlds and institutions. But cosmopolitanization is a highly ambivalent process and does not mean that we are all becoming cosmopolitans. To a certain extent it has led to greater worldwide renationalization and re-ethnification. As a result, the balance between particular attachments and universal orientations needs to be renegotiated.

The media are also undergoing cosmopolitanization. Human rights politics is put into action when the sight of suffering leads to political action intended to lessen the suffering of others. This is only possible when a language is shared that makes the suffering of others understandable. For the current suffering of others to be made comprehensible it must be integrated into a cognitive structure that is connected to the memory of other people's suffering. In this way, earlier catastrophes become relevant in the present and can determine a future that is articulated outside the parameters of the nation-state. However, there are communal boundaries to this globalized compassion. The recognition that compassion and rights are bound to communities and the needs of people in concrete settings is the starting point for a cosmopolitan methodology. In this context, Linklater (2007) suggests that in addition to an embodied cosmopolitanism, which corresponds to Turner's notion of vulnerability, there must also be an "embedded cosmopolitanism."

It was Roger Silverstone (2007) who turned these insights into a complex media theory of moral and political space. He calls the new political space in which morality (and compassion for human rights) is negotiated "Mediapolis." Silverstone's approach to the media rests on Hannah Arendt's analysis of political space, which is not bound to geography. It is the space in which people come together to act and speak. It is an open space in which different narratives circulate. For Silverstone, it is the space where a new morality is made possible. But Silverstone does not talk about a unified worldview. The cosmopolitan is constantly moving between the universal and the particular. It is about plural experiences, and this plurality in turn depends on the unique and the particular. This is how the global media relate to the politics of human rights. It involves a moral minimalism that cannot be reduced to culture and nation. The moral space created by the media presupposes a universalistic minimum involving a number of substantive norms that must be upheld at all costs. The principle that women and children should not be sold or enslaved, the principle that people should be able to speak freely about God or their government without being tortured or killed—these principles are so self-evident that no violation of them is tolerated.

We can speak of a "cosmopolitan common sense" when we have good reasons to assume that a majority of human beings would be willing to defend these minimum universal norms wherever they have force, if called upon to do so (see also Beck and Sznaider 2006, 19). This common sense is created through the power of stories and their visualization. This is the defining mechanism of media that know how to tell and show stories of "you and me"—"human interest" stories. This storytelling capacity is also a burden, since the stories need to be understood, which means that they need to be told under commonsense assumptions. This brings us back to the particular and the communal, as media representations need to swing between the universalistic minimum and a common understanding of it. The overriding importance of the local context remains in place. People do not simply identify with what they

see on television. Strong identifications are produced only when distant events have local resonance. Paradoxically, this ethnocentric focus
on events is precisely what causes a belief in, and a willingness to act
on, universal values. The basis of a wider shared morality is identification with distant others, which is produced through a connection of the
global with the local.

We are, of course, aware that this can have the opposite effect and
result in emotional distancing. Examples abound of how selective perceptions and hence memories can be; one need only think of Africa as
the "forgotten continent," or the millions of children who starve to death
there every year. Paradoxically, it is the global media that make us aware
of the limits of global compassion as well. The circle of those in need of
compassion is expanding, and people in need are forced to compete for
the attention of the global audience. Viewers' attention span is short,
whereas the lists of victims keep growing. Thus, de-territorialized compassion is not evenly distributed directly and equally to all victims. It
does, however, open up a global forum that under certain circumstances
can make people aware of the suffering of others as well as awaken memories of the world's failure to address suffering in the past. Human rights
have become a clear-cut means of gaining legitimacy in the eyes of the
international community. Consequently, paying lip service to solidarity
has been replaced by a normative injunction that developed democracies
find hard to defy. Cosmopolitan memory, which is often the source of
distanced compassion in the first place, is a by-product of news about
others' pain and suffering. Such news may seem cynical when it appears
alongside mass-marketing ads and entertainment programs, but to make
an apathetic public compassionate, one must know how much suffering
it is able and willing to confront.

THEORIZING HUMAN RIGHTS

We draw on Hannah Arendt's contention that for rights to be taken seriously they need political support. Without power, rights are no more than
genteel utterances. But without such words, there would be no rights.

Ours is a political sociology of rights that demonstrates how human rights cannot draw on their metaphysical appeal alone but are primarily conveyed and concretized through negative experiences, especially the memory of past failures to address human rights abuses. We attempt to make memory relevant to our grasp of both the changing tides of human rights and the related sociological theorizing. We need to acknowledge its metaphysical dimension but move beyond a philosophical normative focus. In the case of human rights, mnemonic practices are firmly embodied in historical references and institutional manifestations.

A social theory of human rights that goes beyond assumptions of nationally bound concepts has yet to be constructed. Bryan Turner's pioneering works on human rights (1993, 1997, 2006) are an important step in this direction. Turner does not start with ideas and concepts but with the human body and its vulnerability. It is the body that constitutes the universal aspect of our existence. According to Turner, "vulnerability defines our humanity and is presented here as the common basis of human rights" (2006, 1). Our ontological security, negated by our awareness of universal human frailty, is a major causal factor in the increasing awareness of human rights. But this hardly suffices to ensure the equal enforcement of such broadly defined rights. Enforcement requires social institutions, which themselves are "fragile and precarious, and there is a complex interaction between our human frailty, institution building, and political or state power" (1). Turner recognizes that the balance between universal and particular commitments can, but need not necessarily, be mutually exclusive. Vulnerability in this view becomes the new global condition, mediated by constant access to the sight of suffering people across the world (Boltanski 1999; Tester 1999). People become witnesses to human rights violations. If human rights violations come to be understood as violations of rights based on the commonness of our vulnerability, people will feel that they are defending the foundations of their own vulnerable identities when they defend the importance of human rights for foreigners and strangers. The cultural and political diversity that is essential to this kind of life has been slowly elevated to a global political norm and seems at times to be valued more highly than the particular principle of exclusivity with which it now shares conceptual and political space, judging from the negative reactions to affirmations of national interest in many European states.

Turner's shift from the soul to the body is a sociological attempt to escape this intellectual quagmire. His critique of social constructivism is countered by Malcolm Waters, who argues that "an adequate sociological theory of human rights must, indeed, take a social-constructionist point of view, that human rights is an institution that is specific to a cultural and historical context just like any other, and that its very universality is itself a human construction. The construction of human rights demonstrably transpires in the field of politics and its institutionalization is an emergent arrangement that reflects prevailing balances of political interests" (1996, 593). The Turner-Waters exchange directs our attention to a key omission in sociological analysis, and their theoretical foray presents a formidable starting point from which to elaborate the conceptual significance of human rights in general and its relationship to sovereignty in particular.

An early attempt to construct a sociology of human rights that recognizes the precarious relationship of particular (i.e., national) citizenship and universal (i.e., global) human rights can be found in Hannah Arendt's more politically engaged works, most notably *The Origins of Totalitarianism*. Published in 1951, after Arendt had emigrated to the United States, the book was written very much under the influence of the Holocaust. In a chapter entitled "The Perplexities of the Rights of Men," Arendt reflects on the particular Jewish experience of political "worldlessness" and ends her criticism with a reflection on universal human and citizen rights. Looking from within the prism of the Jewish experience, she addresses one of the key questions of our times: that of minorities and citizenship. Arendt sees the constant constitution of ever new minorities in ethnically homogenous nation-states and therefore views citizenship based on nationality as an ever widening gap in a universal claim to humanity and human rights. Arendt refers to Edmund Burke, who had nothing but contempt for abstract human rights in his criticism of the French Revolution, and extolled the rights of Englishmen. For Arendt, the implication is that without institutional and political protection, universal rights are just empty words, naked, like human beings without citizenship or state protection. The moment the nation-state declines, human rights become nothing but words. Human rights—especially in the shadow of the somber period in which she wrote—could no longer in her view be founded on abstract principles. For Arendt, human rights are not a function of good will or a profound grasp of the truth of things. She primarily addressed the issue of what happens when rightlessness becomes the normal state of affairs (Isaac 1996; Birmingham 2006).

This led her to the conclusion that rights matter only when they are sustained by a political foundation. Men cannot appeal to other men as men, but only as members of communities. This was her sociological insight into the abstractness of human rights. National sovereignty, which might have been instrumental in creating states based on rights in the eighteenth century, turned into the reverse principle, which created a lack of rights for many groups in the twentieth century. We address the complicated relationship of minority and human rights below. Suffice it to say here that the Jews after World War II became the prime symbol of this trap of national sovereignty. While many new states were founded on the territory of the crumbling empires, these states were based on an ethnic concept of nationhood, which automatically excluded those who did not belong to the ethnic core. The consequence was statelessness, and this statelessness brought worldlessness and rightlessness in its wake, since, in Arendt's view, people have to belong to some kind of political community to be fully human. Thus the Jewish fate after the Nazi rise to power became the paradigmatic situation of naked man.

After she came to the United States, Arendt published an essay in 1943 called "We Refugees" that reflected on her own refugee status, in which she wrote, "If we should start telling the truth that we are nothing but Jews, it would mean that we expose ourselves to the fate of human beings who, unprotected by any specific law or political convention, are nothing but human beings. I can hardly imagine an attitude more dangerous, since we actually live in a world in which human beings as such have ceased to exist for quite a while" (reprinted in Arendt 2007, 273). Arendt's interest in the Jewish fate in modern times was also a yardstick for the fate of man in modernity as such (see also Bernstein 1996).

Arendt exposed the limits of abstract universalism, pointing to the necessity to embed and endow human rights with institutional powers. The predicament Arendt depicted circumscribes the dilemma of a social theory of human rights: the discrepancy between the sincerity of declarations that human beings are endowed with universal human rights and the situation of those who lack such rights themselves. To be nothing but human is the greatest danger of all. For Arendt, "abstract," "universal," and "human" are empty terms in a world where people are deprived of the protection of the state or any other institution. Arendt returned the problem of human rights to its political backbone of enforcement and active political engagement on a transnational level. Enforcement is about the social and political foundations of human rights and not about power interests alone. Two aspects of Arendt's analysis are crucial to our argument, namely, the foundations of membership and the conditions for enforcing membership rights. More specifically, our historical-sociological analysis highlights the contingent nature of the link between general human rights and those who have specific rights. Here, "membership precedes recognition, indeed it is the ontological condition of being human, and thus must be the foundation of any and all rights" (Somers and Roberts 2008, 7).

These foundations have changed considerably, however, since the end of the cold war and in the context of global interdependencies. Over the past sixty years there have been numerous challenges to the particularistic presuppositions that inform the dispensation of rights based on one's national status. Humanity is no longer the same abstract powerless category that Arendt saw in the 1940s and 1950s. Human rights are now firmly recognized by both states and international bodies, and are embedded within a set of global expectations about their legal enforcement. Again, the point is not to suggest that this necessarily or always shields humans from violation of their rights (neither do citizenship rights always guarantee this kind of inviolability). Rather, we argue that in the global context human rights have become an institutionalized system that produces values and constitutes interests through the conferral of political legitimacy that can no longer be confined to the nation-state. Here and now the abstract nature of humanity or human rights norms is no longer an impediment to protection but rather has become a necessary condition for mobilizing political support for it.

Turner, for instance, suggests that "the protection offered by nation-states and national citizenship is declining, and yet the state and citizenship remain important for the enforcement of both social and human rights" (2006, 2). Recognizing the impact of globalization, Turner advocates a sociology of rights that concedes the limitations of concepts of bounded citizenship. Social rights of nation-states are complemented by human rights that respond to new global conditions (Soysal 1994). Human rights as a global issue are, of course, not a new phenomenon. Their origins can be traced back to the late eighteenth century and they were formalized internationally starting in the late nineteenth century. Their beginnings are "marked by attempts to extend the processes of delimiting public power to the international sphere, and by attempts thereafter to transform the meaning of legitimate political authority from effective control to the maintenance of basic standards or values, which no political agent, whether a representative of a government or state, should, in principle, be able to abrogate" (Held 2003, 165). Nevertheless, until recently both entitlement and enforcement remained closely tied to national membership.

What has changed, spurred on by globalized imaginations, is the emergence of a cultural and legal recognition of humanity as a meaningful category of membership, not solely in a normative sense but in a political, cultural, and legally consequential terminology which is in line with denationalized concepts of membership. Exclusion from the nation is no longer synonymous with exclusion from the protection of the state. The modern human rights regime is premised on the notion that the prevention of human suffering takes precedence over the principle of sovereignty (Dunne and Wheeler 1999; Ignatieff 2001b), even if prevention of suffering can clash with the state's obligation to provide security for its citizens alone. This is neither a necessary nor an irreversible process. One key reason for this change is that the sanctity of the nation-state is no longer absolute, and both individuals and (ethnic) minorities have obtained a stronger legal status under the aegis of transnational jurisdiction.

We are obviously not suggesting that this implies a decline in human rights violations. They are still with us, and it could be argued that nothing has changed except the rhetoric about human rights. The crux of our argument, however, is that legitimate national interest itself must now be articulated through a powerful cultural depiction and institutional realization of human rights. Here the formation of the modern human rights regime both reflects and contributes to the dissemination and global reach of human rights norms. With the emergence of a human rights regime and its juridical impact during the past two decades, driven largely by the continuous transposition of cosmopolitan memories of failures to prevent human rights abuses, the conditions of membership and enforcement have noticeably been altered.

We thus seek to reconcile the apparent tension between the boundedness of sociological theory in terms of its methodological nationalism as well as the boundaries of social groups and the indivisible nature of human rights treating humans as a generic category through the analytic prism of cosmopolitan memories. Rather than address particular and universal precepts as mutually exclusive categories, we contextualize them by showing how adherence to human rights has become a core legitimating principle of sovereignty itself. More specifically, we examine how the discourse on human rights has developed into a political, cultural, and legal force through a series of mnemonic transpositions about human rights abuses. No longer are these construed solely as universal interdictions; rather, they are often articulated through memories of particular experiences. Cosmopolitanization here consists of how memories of failures to prevent human rights abuses are continually invoked as precedents in both legal and cultural settings. International law and the corresponding human rights legislation draw on particular historical instances, as do political and cultural justifications to establish human rights as the principal source of the legitimacy of state sovereignty. Accordingly, these cosmopolitanized memories contribute substantially to the reconfiguration of sovereign legitimacy and the scope of political responsibility.

As our historical account in chapters 4 through 7 shows, the salience of cosmopolitan memories is closely tied to the end of the cold war and its postutopian implications. In a famous essay entitled "The Liberalism of Fear" (1989), Judith Shklar makes an insightful distinction that applies to this historical juncture.[1] Borrowing from Ralph Waldo Emerson's 1841 essay "The Conservative," Shklar distinguishes between the "party of memory" and the "party of hope." Memory here is not merely a vehicle for the transmission of knowledge but a framework for creating an awareness of past evils. Memory ensures that the permanent stain of past rights abuses serves as a reminder of the human potential for evil. For Shklar, a focus on too much hope, including utopian visions, carries the danger that we might become forgetful of the evils of the twentieth century, which persist in the form of human rights violations. These are the memories of a world in disarray and the constant possibility that civilized society is nothing more than a flimsy veneer. Thus, human rights cannot be grounded in nature, since nature has played too many cruel tricks on humankind. Human rights must be grounded in the dystopian consciousness of a fragile world. Politics thus attempts to prevent the worst from happening.

What matters for our purpose is neither the ontological status of bodily frailty nor the instrumental aspects of human rights. What is more important is the recognition, mediated through cosmopolitan memories of past abuses, of the body's universality as it becomes inscribed in popular imagination and legal doctrine. This is evidenced in the institutionalization of human rights with a concomitant juridification of politics. We do not want to start from an abstract notion of political interests, be they grounded in either power or capital, but show how, once institutionalized, human rights idioms themselves constitute political interests by shaping power balances, and by extension the contours of sovereignty.

SOVEREIGNTY AND HUMAN RIGHTS:
THE HOBBESIAN CHALLENGE

There is a long-standing tradition in Western political thought of differences of opinion on the relationship between rights and sovereignty. Following Hobbes and the social contract theories, and in the aftermath of the French Revolution, the debate between Thomas Paine and Edmund Burke remains an instructive example of sociological discourse. According to Paine's *The Rights of Man* (1791), there is no contradiction between rights and sovereignty. Free individuals transfer sovereignty to an authority (i.e., the government) for the protection of their rights. Paine's essay was an answer to Edmund Burke's criticism of the French Revolution and its notion of abstract rights. For Burke, a government commands people's obedience because it exists as a community of memory beyond the lives of individuals. It is "a partnership not only between those who are living, but between those who are living, those who are dead, and those who are to be born" (Burke 1790/1998, 96). For Burke, historical memory, perceived in terms of continuity, provides legitimacy for sovereignty. Paine subscribed to the opposite view: "It is the living and not the dead who are to be accommodated" (1791/1985, 64). Despite their differences, Paine and Burke shared the notion that contractual obligations are involved in the relationship of a specific community and a particular state (on these obligations, see also Booth 2001). This was the birth of modern nationalism and sociology, which shifted the idea of the nation as a collection of followers to that of an institution that reconciled free-dom and determinism (Beck and Sznaider 2006, 21). Shared historical memories provided a crucial mechanism through which these nations were invented and imagined. In the framework of the Paine-Burke argu-ment, only the sovereign people were considered the principal embodi-ment of rights, and the nation-state was seen as its guarantor.

Sovereignty is a central organizing principle that shapes collectivities' cultural and political knowledge. According to this Aristotelian precept, states are vested with moral imperatives that justify sovereignty. How, then, can we combine an institutional approach with moral sentiments that are not natural but are based on memories of catastrophes? To gauge the strength of human rights on the basis not only of reason but also of sentiments requires a brief corrective to the dominant perspective that reduces the cultural relevance of human rights to the foundations of the continental French and German Enlightenment. Underlying this mis-conception are two different bodies of Enlightenment thought and their respective interpretations of reason and sentiments. Rather than view the rejection of human suffering as some kind of master narrative that emanates from a Kantian conception of reason, or a top-down civilizing process, compassion for and attention to the suffering of others actually originated in the Scottish Enlightenment (Sznaider 2001; Hunt 2007). The text most people think of as the platform of modern human rights campaigns is Kant's "On Perpetual Peace," published in 1795. Kant's idea was that a stable and peaceful political order could only be constructed out of nation-states that made mutually supportive vows of noninterven-tion. This view was embodied to a large degree in the League of Nations and in the original UN charter, and can be considered in many ways to be the seed of the idea of modern international law. There is no escaping that Kant's project regards the sovereignty of nation-states as sacrosanct. It is the central principle on which the entire structure is based. In the post–cold war world, this is precisely the view that human rights cam-paigns reject, as we show in greater detail below.

Contemporary human rights politics starts from the accepted and now legally codified assumption that sovereignty is no longer inviola-ble. Rather, the highest principle is human well-being, and the greatest obligation is to prevent suffering wherever it occurs. Kant's system, based on mutually respected sovereignty, has been sidelined: if interventions are necessary to achieve this goal, sovereignty has to take a backseat. This form of reasoning was embodied in the Scottish Enlightenment, and specifically in the idea that duties are imposed by sympathy and benevolence, motivated by exposure to heart-wrenching stories. The Scots developed a theory of "moral sense," addressing the problem of compassion. They considered "natural compassion" descriptive of human nature as well as normative (Hume 1751/1988; Smith 1759/1998). Human beings both have, and ought to have, fellow feelings for others. As an automatic mechanism for the common good, sympathy is thus seen to lie in the very nature of civil society. In this conception, imagination is the key to compassion. Human beings are cruel because they cannot put themselves in the place of those who suffer. One has to imagine how one would feel in another's place.

Like the French Enlightenment, the Scottish Enlightenment also had a political program of reform. But unlike the French, its proponents did not place all their faith in the sole medium of reason and the wisdom of state officials. They argued instead that the social conditions that fostered sympathy were greater wealth, greater interaction, and greater equality, and that all of these conditions would be enhanced by the growth of the market. In other words, they argued that market cosmopolitanism and moral cosmopolitanism were mutually supportive. Thus it is perhaps not surprising that the human rights regime began to take shape after the end of the cold war, along with the spread of neoliberalism. That this mercantile outlook would in turn produce a form of human rights activism targeting the market as a major source of social and economic human rights violations is only another twist in the conditionality of human rights. Cosmopolitanism, not unlike human rights, is frequently viewed as a realization of the Enlightenment project. In this view, both are universalistic aspirations predicated on a rather narrow continental European interpretation. As much as enlightened thinking is important for the philosophical underpinnings of human rights, it has remained confined to the European context of intellectual cosmopolitanism. Rather than restrict cosmopolitanism to its Enlightenment articulations, we

would like to elaborate on a distinction between its universal aspirations and a more localized manifestation of cosmopolitanism (Cheah
and Robbins 1998). The brief dream of a world society that flourished
in the Enlightenment was crushed by the nationalism to which it simultaneously gave birth, and Enlightenment sensibilities were ineffec-
tual in diminishing war. Yet it was the experience of nationalism in its
most extreme form that gave human rights its potential to flourish. Not
abstract rational thought about how the world ought to work, but human
experiences and memories of catastrophe—which is the experience of
a world where human rights are suspended—constituted the basis for
new human rights regimes.

To base human rights on sentiment rather than on reason needs more
justification. Obviously the rise and spread of cosmopolitan ideas always
has social and political underpinnings. This is often less obvious when
we concentrate on the abstract philosophy of the Enlightenment. If we
look closer, we will find that Enlightenment thinkers did indeed have a
political program for encouraging the spread of cosmopolitan ideas and
institutions: it was, primarily, to get the ear of an enlightened despot.
There are at least two problems with this approach from our contemporary viewpoint. The first is that we now consider despotism by definition
unenlightened. The second is that even on its own terms, it did not work.
Enlightenment cosmopolitanism may have adorned the courts of European monarchs, but it did not spread among the people.

This raises a second point, namely, how cosmopolitan ideas can
spread to people at different levels of society. One theory is that philosophy can become religion (Durkheim 1912/1965). As we discussed
in chapter 2, this process materializes through the sacralization of
memories of human rights abuses. This is what we refer to as rooted
cosmopolitanism producing new forms of localism that are open to
the world. By rooted cosmopolitanism we mean universal values that
descend from the level of pure abstract philosophy and engage people
emotionally in their everyday lives. It is by becoming symbols of people's
personal identities that cosmopolitan philosophy turns into a political
force. By embodying philosophy in rituals, such identities are created,
reinforced, and integrated into communities. A commitment to global

or cosmopolitan values does not imply that cosmopolitans are rootless individuals who prefer humanity over concrete human beings (Appiah 2006). This need not be the case, since global values are embedded in concrete rituals (Turner 2006). War crime trials exemplify such rituals, given the extensive media and scholarly attention they receive.

This emotive dimension is also a crucial element for some of the shared assumptions that guided the cosmopolitan reactions to the catastrophes of World War II. The Holocaust in particular posed a challenge to the universal Enlightenment premises of reason and rationality. Paradoxically, the Holocaust functioned simultaneously as the source for a critique of Western universalism and the foundation for a cosmopolitan desire to propagate human rights universally. The central question here is whether the Holocaust is part of modernity or the opposite, a return to barbarism representing the breakdown of modernity—a question connected to the broader debate about whether barbarism constitutes a separate breakdown of civilization or whether it is very much part of modern rationalization and bureaucratization itself. According to Theodor Adorno and Max Horkheimer's study *The Dialectic of Enlightenment* (1944), barbarism is an immanent quality of modernity, not its corruption. In their view, civilizational ruptures, at least potentially, relate to the processes of rationalization and bureaucratization that characterize modernity.

For Hannah Arendt (1951), the Nazis represented the breakdown of the Enlightenment and democracy, critical judgment and reason. The ambivalence between the above-mentioned frames of civilization and barbarism remained the primary organizing principle for Arendt's thoughts on the Holocaust. Nazism, for her, was nothing particularly German but rather a manifestation of totalitarianism. Universalizing the phenomenon did not prevent her from recognizing its singular features. She perceived that the uniqueness of the Holocaust lay not only in the scope and systematic nature of the killings but in the very attempt to deny humanity as such. Conventional categories of crime became irrelevant, a view that was later incorporated into the legal canon through the concept of crimes against humanity. The legal recognition of crimes against humanity means foremost a limitation on sovereignty. States cannot act as they please. Even state legislation cannot be considered anymore the last ground of legitimacy. A crime against humanity means that there exists a higher authority states need to orient themselves around.

Before examining the codification of these new legal categories, it is instructive to take a closer look at the malleability and historical trajectories of sovereignty. Legitimate statehood is articulated through dominant values that are subject to historical change. "Ancient Greeks tied the moral purpose of the state to the cultivation of *bios politikos*, a distinctive form of communal life; Renaissance Italians defined it in terms of the pursuit of civic glory; Europeans in the age of absolutism linked it to the preservation of a divinely ordained, rigidly hierarchical social order; and in the modern era, the rationale for the state has been increasingly tied to the protection of individuals' rights" (Reus-Smit 2001, 528). What is revealing about this historical analysis is the omission of a key factor for legitimate political authority in the modern state, namely, the protection of the nation. Nationhood, largely propelled through the human rights concept of self-determination, has played a constitutive role in the establishment of sovereignty as a protector of collective rights.

When absolute concepts of sovereignty and human rights are juxtaposed, the primacy of particular sovereignty and the indivisibility of universal human rights are locked into a zero-sum equation (Dunne and Wheeler 1999). Consequently, much of the debate is framed around a dichotomy that stipulates either the persistence of bounded nation-state sovereignty or its erosion. The spatial and cultural presuppositions of sovereignty itself (i.e., the congruence of state, nation, and legitimacy), however, remain for the most part uncontested. Sovereignty and the nation-state continue to be perceived as a coextensive pair rather than as distinct concepts in a malleable relationship. In this view, sovereignty involves the attempted abolition of temporality in favor of spatiality (Walker 1988). But sovereignty is not identical to the concept of the nation, which is usually predicated on a shared culture and not confined to territorial dimensions (Gellner 1983). The convergence (i.e., the coupling of nation and state) occurred at particular historical junctures starting with the French Revolution, greatly expanded toward the end of the nineteenth century, and came into full blossom during the twentieth century. Furthermore, the congruence of nation and state has never been as complete as most theories claimed (Brubaker 1996). Neither has sovereignty been vested with the absolute qualities usually attributed to it (Krasner 1999).

Despite distinctive historical manifestations and varying definitions of modern sovereignty, there has long been a consensus in the sociological literature that it encompasses the idea of a political system in which authority is based on exclusive command over territory and a degree of autonomy (Giddens 1985). This view is echoed in Max Weber's definition of the sovereign state as "a human community that successfully claims the monopoly of the legitimate use of physical force within a given territory" (Weber 1919/1958, 77–78). While this definition says nothing about what constitutes a political community, nationality and ethnicity were the primary reference points for sociological approaches to sovereignty during the twentieth century. This nation-state-centric view resonates with prevalent conceptions in the sociological field, where debates about the concept of sovereignty are largely absent, owing for the most part to dehistoricized and naturalized conceptualizations of sovereignty.

Not surprisingly, memory studies linked to the nation and particular pasts have not been used for an institutional analysis of rights and sovereignty. This omission is also the result of the national caging that coincided with the emergence of sociology in the late nineteenth century. Sociology construed particular memories of nationhood above all as a means of social integration. The triumph of this perspective can be seen in the way the nation and state are frequently treated as interchangeable terms, concealing the historically conditioned nature of political sovereignty.[1] The coextensiveness of nation and state is so ingrained in sociological thought that the topic of sovereignty remains an essentially uncontested concept. Consequently, most studies of sovereignty, even when recognizing the historical malleability of legitimate political authority, continue to view it in categorical terms. Hence the impact of human rights norms on sovereignty is usually addressed in contradictory terms.

Rather than view human rights and sovereignty as mutually exclusive terms, we focus on the constitutive role of human rights norms for the reconfiguration of legitimate statehood. Recent transformations of sovereignty, we suggest, are shaped by processes of cosmopolitanization, leading to a denationalized form of legitimate statehood. State sovereignty remains strong, but its legitimacy now draws on the adherence to new, nation-transcending cultural norms that involve the interaction of universal (cosmos) and particular (polis) orientations. The reconfiguration of sovereignty takes place in a broad context of "global assemblages" (Sassen 2006), which enable the national frame of reference to be permeable to a universal set of cultural meanings.

Cosmopolitanized memories of state failures to prevent human rights abuses pose a direct challenge to Hobbes, who provided the foundational assumptions of modern sovereignty. The shift toward human rights and the concomitant transformation of nation-state sovereignty raise new questions about the Hobbesian quid pro quo of freedom and protection. Hobbes wrote that people's assessment of the degree of security the state can provide is proportional to how insecure they feel. Fear of violent death and the desire for self-preservation led to the acceptance of the Leviathan as the ultimate protector, and this essentially supplied the rationale for the legitimacy of modern state sovereignty (Bourke 2005). The human rights regime also seeks to free people from the fear of violent death. Both the Leviathan and the legitimating power of the human rights regime are predicated on their ability to inspire fear of punishment and violation. Hobbes refers to a "state of nature" characterized by anarchy and war of all against all. His description conjures up imagery of violent death that ultimately explains the delegation of legitimate authority to the state in return for protection. Hobbes's state of nature is a prehistorical construct that asks people to abandon their desire for immortality. Social memories of actual history become significant, however, when states stop being protectors and become violators. The systematic destruction of European Jewry, iconicized in memory as the Holocaust, as well as other forms of genocide, demonstrate that people are not only mortal but can be disposed of at will by a brutal and sovereign state.

The pervasiveness of memories of state-sponsored human rights violations and their legal inscription in the global age have undermined the foundational Hobbesian contract. In particular, memories of the Holocaust underscore the fact that the state does not provide security and that in some cases the Leviathan can become the biggest executioner of all (Levy and Sznaider 2001). People obey the state because fear of violent death supplants fear of the state. After 1945, at least in the western European context, memories of chaos and civil war and the constant fear of violent death were the root cause for the shift of some legitimacy to nation-transcending (i.e., human rights) principles. Encouraged by the American presence in western Europe and triggered by the rationale of the cold war, alternative notions of (citizenship) rights emerged to challenge the national premises of solidarity, long cultivated through memories of war and bloodshed. These have now been replaced by the global market as the European Union began as an economic unity pact, mutual interdependence, consumerism, and mutual indifference, as well as ethnic and religious identification (Sznaider 2001).

In the final analysis, the ascendance of a human rights regime is nothing but Leviathan writ large (Levy and Sznaider 2004). Unlike Hobbes's imaginary state of nature, the human rights narrative is based on historical memories. But, like Hobbes, it ultimately leans toward an abstract scenario that is less about actual abuses than about a new illusion of protection. There is no space for barbarous acts to be treated as normal occurrences and become part of, say, the daily news. Here the commemoration of the Holocaust as a universal code for human rights abuses is ultimately about forgetting the particular experience and redirecting the focus to symbolic political and cultural practices that underscore the (re) solutions offered by the human rights regime, rather than engaging with the historical event itself. Here, too, it is the unbearable need to cope with particular forms of violations and violence that must make room for our desire for security and protection. In other words, the politics of memory that universalizes human rights is frequently predicated on an ahistorical dimension similar to Hobbes's state of nature.

At the turn of the twenty-first century, global processes are creating numerous challenges, both to the territorial premises of sovereignty and to the particularistic presuppositions that inform the dispensation of rights based on national affiliation. The transformation of citizenship in many European countries is one indication of these changes. Migratory trends in the second half of the twentieth century have contributed to new patterns of claim making that transcend conventional appeals to nationality, by invoking human rights conventions and demanding the recognition of minority group rights. This global component is echoed in the emergence of postnational trends (Soysal 1994), which are characterized by a decoupling of rights and identity. Membership rights are no longer dispensed solely on the basis of particular national attributes but are increasingly derived from the universal status of personhood.

These nation-transcending features of human rights are not only changing the twentieth-century premises of citizenship; they are also affecting the coordinates of sovereignty. The supremacy of particular sovereignty and the indivisibility of universal human rights are often perceived as mutually exclusive categories. Such a view is not surprising when we consider that human rights render the implicit limitations of sovereignty explicit. While states can choose to enforce or ignore human rights at their peril, they are not the sole judges of the content of human rights laws. However, rather than presuppose that globalization, or a universal rights discourse, necessarily leads to the demise of sovereignty, we suggest that an increasingly denationalized concept of legitimacy contributes to a reconfiguration of sovereignty itself. This kind of denationalized concept of legitimacy is mediated by the texture of historical memories, and hence lends renewed urgency to the Paine-Burke debate.

Sovereignty has proved to be an enduring concept, capable of mutating by adjusting to different political, cultural, and economic circumstances. Just as the absolutist states envisioned by Hobbes differed greatly from democratic parliamentary entities since the nineteenth century, post-twentieth-century globalization is reconfiguring the meaning of sovereignty once again. Global processes have eroded the boundaries of the sovereign nation-state by challenging many of the monopolies set up by the modern state between the mid-nineteenth and mid-twentieth century (Albrow 1996; Giddens 1985). These global developments are frequently interpreted as a sign of the demise of sovereignty (Ohmae 1990; Strange 1996). Ironically, despite these developments (or perhaps precisely because of them), Carl Schmitt's 1922 dictum in his *Political Theology* that the sovereign is "the one who can proclaim a state of exception"

(5) has recently regained popularity. Following this line of thought, Giorgio Agamben (2005) claims that affairs of sovereignty are increasingly usurped by the executive power and do not allow for any interference.[2]

The analysis presented here takes the position that the idea of fixed territorial boundaries functioning "as the natural repository of political legitimacy" (Gellner 1983, 55) is the product of a specific historical-political process, which is now being challenged by the global dissemination of human rights norms. The transformative power of human rights is predicated on the recent uncoupling of nation and state, which is mediated by distinctive memories of past human rights abuses and their institutionalization in a cosmopolitan legal order. By treating state and nation synonymously, many scholars confound the fact that the state remains a central entity as an indicator of unchanged sovereignty. However, globalization questions the fit between nation-state and society (Beck 2001; Scholte 2000). Saskia Sassen, for instance, observes this partial unbundling as follows: "One of the features of the current phase of globalization is that the fact a process happens within the territory of a sovereign state does not necessarily mean that it is a national process. Conversely, the national (such as firms, capital, culture) may increasingly be located outside the national territory, for instance, in a foreign country or digital spaces. This localization of the global, or of the non-national, in national territories, and of the national outside national territories, undermines a key duality running through many of the methods and conceptual frameworks prevalent in the social sciences, that the national and the non-national are mutually exclusive" (2000, 145–46). As a result, denationalized political and cultural spaces become possible.

Ernest Gellner's definition of the modern nation-state as "primarily a political principle, which holds that the political and the national unit should be congruent" (1983, 1), is thus historically contingent and subject to revision. To be sure, this reassessment of nationhood varies a great deal, and is particularly salient in the European context. The diminishing normative return of the national depends to a large extent on the specific political expediencies collectivities face. Since the history of state sovereignty varies according to perspectives that are themselves historically situated in discursive spaces defined by the principle of sovereignty (Walker 1988, 18ff.), the decoupling of nation and state must be examined in light of its contemporary manifestations.

Accordingly, our historical analysis focuses on the emergence of the cosmopolitan memory tropes that challenge nation-state-centered memories in the European context. The conventional concept of collective memory is nationally bounded, and this national container is slowly showing fissures. Particular national and ethnic memories are not erased but transformed. They continue to exist, but globalization processes shape the balance of (universal) human rights–oriented and (particular) nation-centric memories, informing the parameters of sovereignty.

The political clout of human rights remains conditional (Henkin 1999). Transformations of warfare and terrorism, among other things, can explain the fragility of the human rights regime because they thrust the state back to its Hobbesian foundations, namely, the provision of security for its citizens. As we discuss in the following chapters, new security threats, the breakdown of states, and other developments operate as stark reminders of the precarious nature of the human rights regime. The salience of human rights norms is a function of how memories of human rights abuses and fears of violent death contend with each other. We return to this point in greater detail in our concluding chapter on the post-9/11 tension between terrorism/antiterrorism and human rights as yet another moment in the reconfiguration of the relationship of state sovereignty and human rights.

4

INTERNATIONAL LAW AND THE FORMATION
OF NATION-STATES

As we showed in chapter 3, human rights as a global issue are not, of course, a new phenomenon. Their roots can be traced back to the late eighteenth century, and the beginning of their international formalization to the late nineteenth century. However, this was neither a linear nor a predetermined process, but one that involved many twists and turns caught between moral ideals and their institutionalization. As David Held observes, this institutionalization was "marked by attempts to extend the processes of delimiting public power to the international sphere, and by attempts thereafter to transform the meaning of legitimate political authority from effective control to the maintenance of basic standards or values, which no political agent, whether a representative of a government or state, should, in principle, be able to abrogate" (2003, 165). This does not mean that power politics and interests are the only movers of this process. Nor is the history of human rights evolutionary. Rather, it is characterized by discontinuities that relate to a series of radical experiments that came to be remembered as failures but are commemorated as holding the potential for a better future. The evidence can be found in nation-states' efforts to "civilize" themselves through binding conventions.

Many of today's human rights conventions go back to the Geneva Conventions of 1864 and 1906, the Hague Conventions of 1899 and 1907, and the Geneva Conventions of 1929 and 1949. Each can be viewed as the product of memories of previous failures to combat human rights abuses. Starting in the mid-nineteenth century, these interstate conventions were complemented by the actions of INGOs, with limited resources and authority, representing "humanity" vis-à-vis states (Boli and Thomas 1997, 172). This ushered in a new kind of global politics in terms of rights for women (Berkovitch 1999), children, and animals (Sznaider 2001). The presence of INGOs also circumscribed state sovereignty in terms of rules of warfare and weaponry (Held 2003). Characterizing the link between human rights and sovereignty were efforts on a universal scale to extend the rights of formerly excluded members of civil society (women, children, animals, enemies in war). This trend began in the nineteenth century and continues today. It is part of a larger civilization process (Elias 1969) that aims to safeguard the rights of minorities against increasingly nationalist and ethnic collectives, such as the enclaves that reshaped the imperial system after World War I (Fink 2004; Mazower 1999).

This process traces its origins to the French Revolution, which combined the rights of man with national sovereignty as a discourse of rights that revolved around the extension of citizenship privileges (see also Hunt 2007; Moyn 2007). It was this kind of revolution, which identified the people with the state, that would be shattered later on with the political mobilization of ethnic and national minorities. Whereas the human rights regime today contributes to the uncoupling of nation and state, human rights at the outset were closely entwined with legitimating the nation as a source of sovereignty. Rights became part of the self-definition of the state and its subjects, rather than developing a momentum of their own that was no longer bound by membership in a particular group. The greater ties between nation and state were further sanctioned in the aftermath of World War I, when, after the collapse of the Habsburg and Ottoman empires in central and southern Europe, ethnic minorities sought state protection. The collapse of the European order created a new category of people, the ethnic minority living within a nation-state's borders (Mazower 1999). This is an important feature to bear in mind, for our current familiarity with minorities can be misconstrued as a long-standing universal phenomenon. This ahistorical perception has frequently led to a conflation of minority rights with human rights terminology, the latter being shaped by events during the second half of the twentieth century. In fact, the distinction between nations (majorities) and minorities is a rather recent one. When the nation-state (a Western principle) was introduced in the former territories of nineteenth-century empires throughout eastern, central and southern Europe, the existence of large contingents of minorities became inevitable. Thus a system of protection was imposed on these new states—a feature resented from the start by new entities such as Poland and Czechoslovakia.

The treaties that settled World War I gave sixty million people states of their own and turned another twenty-five million into minorities. With the fall of the old empires, national minorities had to search for political and social solutions to their volatile postimperial status (Brubaker 1996). Their rights were not protected by national states but rather by a newly constituted international institution, the League of Nations, which was envisioned as an international utopia based on the equality of nations under international law (Pedersen 2007). The minority rights protections system contained a moral impetus, namely, the desire to make international relations conform to a higher morality rather than be governed by amorality. The League of Nations sought to create a political structure that would come to terms with national aspirations but did not surrender to them completely. International law was supposed to keep these aspirations in check (Koskenniemi 2004). As the victorious powers assembled in 1918–19 to make peace in Europe, news of the massacres in eastern Europe reminded everyone that peace and stability in the new successor states of the fallen empire depended on the way in which minorities in those states would be protected (Fink 2004; Mazower 2004). The emergence of highly exclusionist politics during the 1920s and 1930s evidently made this a futile undertaking. The primacy of national sovereignty trumped the rights of minorities, and the League of Nations had few instruments to enforce compliance of any sort. In that postimperial context there was a pervasive sense that the nation-state could not protect its minorities who were of a different nationality. As Arendt, whose thinking on totalitarianism was strongly informed by these perplexities, put it, "the nation had conquered the state" (1951, 275). Behind this concept lies a clear-cut notion of sovereignty that does not allow external restraints to dictate how states should regulate their internal affairs.

Although World War I constituted a temporary setback to internationalist ideals, it also served as a catalyst for renewed efforts to preserve the nation-state as an international principle. This dilemma was clearly set out in President Woodrow Wilson's speech on the Fourteen Points on January 8, 1918, a proposal that was intended to end World War I (and all wars) and signified the entry of the United States onto the global political scene as part of the nascent League of Nations. Point 14 stated that "a general association of nations must be formed under specific covenants for the purpose of affording mutual guarantees of political independence and territorial integrity to great and small states alike." Beyond the imperatives of power politics, Wilson believed in an ideal system that Thomas Knock (1995) termed "progressive internationalism." Wilson thus inaugurated the political beginnings of contemporary trends in which international politics are informed by moral and legal principles and in which, by extension, human rights abuses are subject to international treaties. However, and this is the crucial difference between the international ethos then and the cosmopolitan outlook now, these measures were designed to support the nation-state, leaving the sanctity of national sovereignty untouched. In contradistinction to recent cosmopolitanization, the international arena remained focused on domestic ideas and the relationship between nations, and was designed to reproduce the principles of nation-state sovereignty. Wilson's proposals for minority rights for the postimperial ethnic minorities of eastern and southeastern Europe, which were articulated at the peace agreements in Paris in 1919 that brought World War I to a close, gave these sociological notions historical reality.

While in current debates minority rights are often conflated with human rights, this was not the case when human rights were codified in the wake of World War II. Quite the contrary: human rights were the "correct" answer to the pervasive memories of failures to protect minorities. In the memory of those who tried to hammer out a new order after World War II especially in Europe, minority rights were the perceived evil of the interwar period, and were even cast as partly responsible for Hitler's aggression and the outbreak of the war.

This is particularly true for Jewish minorities between the wars. In the period before World War II, Jews constantly experienced the tension between universalism and particularism: they were too universal to be particular and too particular to be universal. They were present everywhere without really belonging anywhere. They were living at the "crossroads of the wide open spaces" (Feuchtwanger 1930, 465), for which they would pay a high price. "For almost half a century," Stefan Zweig wrote in his memoirs, "I was educating my heart to beat in a cosmopolitan fashion, like that of a *citoyen du monde*—to no avail. On the very day I lost my passport, I discovered, at age 58, that by losing your homeland, you are losing more than just a fenced-in plot of earth" (1988, 468). Their "nonbelonging" made the Jews the cosmopolitans of Europe but also the defenseless victims of the Nazis. In their experience, place and non-place commixed. The European Jews were assimilated and orthodox, Jewish and not Jewish, national and cosmopolitan, all at the same time. There was only one thing they were not: an integral part of Europe's national societies.

European Jewry called into question the premises of homogeneity, which are always viewed as shaped by and confined within the nation-state: "the homogeneity of space and population, and the homogeneity of past and future" (Beck 2001, 22). Jewish diplomatic activities during the peace conference in 1919 foreshadowed problems to come. Jews fought for their respective countries in World War I, and after the war, when Wilson and the Allies offered national liberation to the peoples of eastern and southern Europe, the fate of the Jews depended on international guarantees (Arendt 1951; Fink 2004). Their lifeworlds had been shaped by premodernity; their integration into the modern world of nation-states had failed. To be able to evolve, Jewish communities were dependent on the niches provided by the multiethnic variety of the now extinct large empires (Diner 2003).

It was not until the advent of the modern concept of the nation-state that previously rather vaguely defined nationalities became ethnically homogenized. The unity of people and territory is a concept unknown to the Jewish religion, however. The transition to a postnational, multiethnic society without territorially bound identities is nothing new to Jews, who have traditionally inhabited comparable lifeworlds. Thus it is no coincidence that the concept of the Diaspora migrated from Jewish theology to transnational cultural studies. Neither time nor space unambiguously defines what it means to be Jewish. At the same time, Jews had to be diplomats without a country, paradigmatically defining a kind of deterritorialized politics of rights. The end of World War I meant constant threats for Jews as an ethnic minority in times of nation-state formation. This threat to Jewish existence has now largely vanished from the memory of Jews and others, subsumed by memories of World War II.

It is precisely this purging of memory that is crucial for a historical sociology of rights, because it illustrates how particular representations of history shape the emergence of rights regimes and their political and cultural relevance. A case in point is how Allied leaders dismissed Jewish claims after the war (Fink 2004). The Allies suspected Jews of Bolshevism but were also very much concerned with the future of German minorities throughout the new nations in eastern and central Europe (MacMillan 2001). Some Zionist leaders who attended the peace conference in fact reinforced this fear when they tried to divide the Jewish delegation and threatened Wilson and others that if their demand for a Jewish homeland was not met, Jewish masses in eastern Europe were likely to embrace the Bolshevists.

The Jews as a collective people became Europe's paradigmatic minority, but the international system created in 1919 could not protect them from the atrocities and destruction they experienced only two decades later. This tremendous failure of minority protection became one of the more significant catalysts for the emergence of the human rights regime in the ruins of World War II. It was a particular memory of a particular group that constituted an entire consciousness of rights after World War II. It may be no coincidence that people like Raphael Lemkin, who coined the term genocide, Hersch Lauterpacht, who first codified the modern concept of human rights, or Hans Kelsen, who revived the legal cosmopolitanism of the Roman Empire, were all Jews who came from the former empires. Toward the end of the war Lauterpacht and Kelsen, as legal scholars, attempted to conceptualize how minority rights might become an integral part of human rights by proposing that minority groups should have the legal personality requisite for submitting claims directly before an international court (Claude 1955, 66; Mazower 2004). These cultural and political tropes continue to haunt the memory of policymakers in the twenty-first century.

Jews were not the only significant minority group. Ethnic Germans, who had been living for centuries in regions of eastern Europe, are another case in point. Their presence became the model par excellence for an irredentist Fifth Column destabilizing Europe in the 1930s. Ethnic Germans became a primary example of conflated memories, of how minorities are remembered as both victims and perpetrators. A related illustration of the way in which memories of minority politics crucially affected the construction of a European future is reflected in the person of Edvard Beneš, a sociologist, politician, president, Czech nationalist, and internationalist who participated in many of the international conferences and set the tone for postwar debates about human rights. His name today is linked primarily to the so-called Beneš decrees, which expelled ethnic Germans from Czechoslovakia after World War II. He published an article in 1942 in *Foreign Affairs* in which he laid out his vision for a postwar Europe, combining, in his words, a "political and moral approach" (1942, 230). The ultimate goal, he suggested, "was to create a confederation of Europe as part of a world commonwealth" (234). Addressing the issue of minority rights, he viewed minorities, particularly the German minorities in Czechoslovakia, as a source of unrest and even as traitors. He condemned the idealistic tendencies of the peacemakers of 1918 who tried to protect minorities: "I observe, therefore, though with regret, that the prewar system for the protection of minorities broke down." And he suggested that "before we begin to define the rights of minorities we must define the rights of majorities and the obligations of minorities" (237). In many ways, Beneš foresaw what would become official international policy only two years later: "It will be necessary after this war to carry out a transfer of populations on a very much larger scale than after the last war. This must be done in as humane a manner as possible, internationally organized and internationally financed" (238). At the end of his essay Beneš concluded that the old League of Nations had not become involved in the internal affairs of its member states. In his view, this had to change: "So the united Europe of the future must find a way to stop the development of absolutism in individual countries in time, before it becomes a public danger. I believe that after the present war a chapter of Human Rights must be constitutionally established throughout the world" (241).

In this seminal essay, which alluded to broader historical trends, the transition and demarcation between minority rights and human rights was set down. Beneš was clearly an interested party in this new order. He wanted a new Czechoslovakia without Germans. He was an active participant with particular memories of the dismantling of his own country by the minority rights treaties. The minority protection system was practically failed history, and in remembering this failure, the powers bowed to Germany's demands and transferred to Germany the area claimed by the German minority in Czechoslovakia at the 1938 Munich conference. Beneš acted as an observer and clearly expressed the spirit of the time. In 1945 he gave an interview to the Jewish Telegraphic Agency in which he expressed his support for a Jewish state while at the same time demanding that the remaining Jews in Czechoslovakia either completely assimilate and obtain equal rights or leave the country (Baron 1945, 10). This was of great concern to surviving Jews in the aftermath of the Holocaust. Many of the protagonists, Lemkin among them, remembered the interwar debacles and were involved in the creation of new human rights initiatives after World War II. The limitations of the international system and the general failures of the League of Nations constitute an important swath of the memories of past failures that led to the creation of the United Nations. Human rights were viewed as independent of governments, but there was no institution outside of government to guarantee them.

REMEMBERING MINORITIES AND THEIR RIGHTS

Debates on minority rights can be derived from historical events (e.g., Mazower 1999; Preece 1998), and they can be grounded in theory (Kymlicka 1996). If we do not want to confuse minority rights and human rights, we must avoid ahistorical considerations that treat minorities in abstract or structural terms. Suffused with present concerns as they inevitably are, minority rights tend to be linked to multiculturalism and the kind of demands groups make of the state. This point is related to a central debate in political theory known as the human rights versus popular sovereignty split (Benhabib 2006). The normative orientation of political theorists seeks to mediate between democracy (popular sovereignty) and liberalism (human rights). Yet this mediation, beyond the theoretical claim that combining the two is rational and therefore universally valid, remains problematic in practice. Rationality, whether as a foundational or a communicative category, even in its current flush of popularity, also entails a reaction that denies its primacy. As a result, many of these theoretical notions regarding minorities, liberalism, and groups are presentist without addressing the ramifications that memories of gross rights violations have for subsequent articulations of human rights.

During the interwar period, two minorities became crucial historical actors and were remembered as such. The first were the Jews who became caught up in the formation of new nation-states in southern and eastern Europe and were active in the formulation and representation of minority rights protection. The primary obstacle they faced was that they did not have a country of their own and became the ultimate victims of an exterminatory fascism. The Jews who survived the Holocaust became refugees who for various reasons could not be repatriated to their countries of origin. They were treated either as a "huddled mass" that needed generalized protection in terms of human rights, or alternatively as a sovereign nation of their own that was recognized by the international community in 1947 and concretized in 1948 with the founding of the state of Israel. Despite the founding of Israel as a constitutional fact, the process of Jewish sovereignty, and the Jewish victim per se, became an archetype of victimhood to be protected by all means by the international community. Jews were to be protected not as Jews but as abstract members of the human race. The central paragraph of the Genocide Prevention Act, defining the "intent to destroy, in whole or in part, a national, ethnical, racial or religious group, as such," speaks exactly to this point. The Jewish victim was turned into a group "as such." This is why, in the politics of memory, ultimate victimhood devoid of sovereignty has become crucial.

The second historical minority group that informs our discussion is the aforementioned ethnic Germans. Like the Jews, they became a tenuous minority as a result of the collapse of the empires. They participated with the Jews in interwar minority politics until the coalition broke down after the Nazis came to power in 1933 (Bamberger-Stemman 2000; Hiden and Smith 2006; Nesemann 2007). German minorities were always considered a group whose loyalties lay elsewhere, since there was a sovereign state that protected their interests. Memories of prewar German minority politics contributed to the transfer of Germany's population from Poland and Czechoslovakia as a necessary, legitimate act intended to stabilize the postwar order. As such, the German minority turned into another archetype: that of the treacherous, untrustworthy minority.

Between these two archetypes lies the historical memory of the Armenians who were killed by the Turks during World War I. Helpless to some, traitors to others, they become another crucial symbolic element in the politics of guilt and responsibility in the modern period. The Armenian case is instructive, as it shows how the transformation of memories is bound up with the general status of human rights values and their frailty, both domestically and internationally. What is particularly striking about the malleability of memories of human rights abuses is that their exclusion from the public realm is often not necessarily a function of official or outright suppression but the result of other political expediencies.

The widespread belief that the massacre of Armenians has long been a taboo subject and has only recently received global attention is erroneous. As early as May 29, 1915, the governments of France, Great Britain, and Russia issued a joint statement in which they denounced the Turkish atrocities against the Armenians as a "crime against humanity," a category usually associated with the later Nuremberg trials.[1] The joint declaration sent to the State Department in Washington reads as follows: "The French Foreign Office requests following notice be given to the Turkish Government. Quote. May 24th: For about a month the Kurd and Turkish populations of Armenia have been massacring Armenians with the connivance and often assistance of Ottoman authorities. Such massacres took place in middle April at Erzerum, Dertchun, Eguine, Akn, Bitlis, Mush, Sassun, Zeitun, and throughout Cilicia. Inhabitants of about one hundred villages near Van were all murdered. In that city Armenian quarter is besieged by Kurds. At the same time in Constantinople Ottoman Government ill-treats inoffensive Armenian population. In view of those new crimes of Turkey against humanity and civilization, the Allied governments announce publicly to the Sublime-Porte that they will hold personally responsible [for] these crimes all members of the Ottoman government and those of their agents who are implicated in such massacres." As a result of pressure from the victorious Allies, leading Turkish politicians were put on trial in Istanbul between 1919 and 1921. This could be considered a precursor to later international tribunals that underscored the significance of human rights values (Bass 2001; Kramer 2001).

Only a few years later, however, Hitler referred to the Turkish atrocities against the Armenians as an example of how easily the world community forgets and how states can mistreat their subjects with impunity. Outlining his own goals, Hitler stated, "Our strength consists in our speed and in our brutality. Genghis Khan led millions of women and children to slaughter—with premeditation and a happy heart. History sees in him solely the founder of a state. It's a matter of indifference to me what a weak western European civilization will say about me. . . . I have issued the command that our war aim does not consist in reaching certain lines, but in the physical destruction of the enemy. Accordingly, I have placed my death-head formations in readiness with orders to them to send to death mercilessly and without compassion, men, women, and children of Polish derivation and language. Only thus shall we gain the living space [Lebensraum] which we need. Who, after all, speaks today of the annihilation of the Armenians?" (quoted in Lochner 1942, 1, 4). This statement is emblematic of both failure on the institutional level and the strength of sovereignty and the marginal role human rights played during the interwar period.

Today there is growing attention to and recognition of the Armenian genocide as a politically charged and scholarly controversial issue. This genocide casts a shadow on international diplomatic relations (especially with respect to Turkey's entry into the EU) and on issues of freedom of speech. What all these minority groups have in common is that they existed as historical groups and both acted and were acted upon. For the members of these communities, memory is indeed ethnicity and has become part of the link between history and the memory of the groups themselves. In the memory of politics and the politics of memory, however, these groups have ceased to be historical actors and have turned into structural generic players who have become the tokens of modern-day rights politics. This trajectory was consolidated and further institutionalized in the aftermath of World War II.

5

FROM MINORITY TO HUMAN:
THE CHANGING FACE OF RIGHTS

COSMOPOLITANISM AND THE SPIRIT OF EUROPE

This chapter addresses the complex relationship between human rights, cosmopolitanism, and sovereignty through three portals: seminal historical events and concomitant memories, related articulations in intellectual controversies, and their respective implementation in the context of legal debates. With memories of the atrocities of World War II and Nazi extermination camps omnipresent, the postwar period constitutes a crucial historical juncture for a renewed articulation of human rights principles and, at least in theory, a more conditional approach to sovereignty derived from a partial discrediting of nationalism in the European context. While emerging geopolitical realities and the nascent cold war would eventually forestall the implementation of human rights, the programmatic statements that emanated from war crime trials and universal declarations in the aftermath of the war nevertheless became the institutional and mnemonic reference points for the subsequent formation of the human rights regime. The postwar period was marked by strong universalism and as espoused by the victors in the war, a liberal rather than a socialist form of universalism, as is evidenced in numerous debates and official declarations on human rights. By privileging a language of human rights, the framers of the post–World War II order essentially agreed to marginalize minority rights conceptions that had dominated the interwar period.

The postwar statements of the German philosopher Karl Jaspers are emblematic of the Eurocentric universalism that also characterizes much of the core European postnational discourse of recent years.[1] Relying on a single voice is always problematic, but Jaspers's position would come to stand for a Germany aligned with the victorious western Allies and embody the new Europeanized German. The American occupying forces considered him the moral voice of the "other Germany." Married to a Jewish woman he refused to divorce, Jaspers lost his academic position in 1937. As the Americans attempted to reform the political culture of Germany, they needed thinkers and academics like Jaspers to assist them in rebuilding the university system. In the aftermath of World War II, Europeanization primarily implied the rebuilding of western Europe with a pacified Germany in its midst, and the image of the United States as a counterweight to Soviet influence in the East. Germany had to be westernized through its integration into a newly formed interdependent system of western European states. Intellectual debates in Germany dealing with guilt and responsibility spearheaded by Jaspers, and issues framed around the realization of Nazi atrocities before and during the war, would four decades later become paradigmatic European debates about the guilt of nations in general (Barkan 2000).

Between 1945 and 1948 Jaspers became a symbol for the American occupying forces. He was German, he did not emigrate, but he was not a Nazi. He could become the symbol of another Germany. The Allies trusted him (Kirkbright 2004). His book on German guilt became a founding document of the new West Germany (see Diner 1997). He saw the postwar era and the Nuremberg trials as a world that needed to be based upon a universal Kantian cosmopolitanism, a world without Others and without borders. Early in 1946 he published a study that would subsequently become a seminal document for the nascent Federal Republic and attempts to come to terms with its past. *Die Schuldfrage* (The Question of German Guilt) sought to refute the notion that Germans were collectively guilty for the crimes committed by the Nazis. Distinguishing between criminal, political, moral, and metaphysical guilt, Jaspers established his view that to condemn a people as a whole violates the claim of being human. It should be noted that Jaspers was not the only voice to address the question of guilt in Germany, but since it seemed to absolve so many Germans from their collusion with the Nazi regime, the distinctions Jaspers put forward became the dominant trope then and is the one remembered today (Olick 2005).

At the same time, his book was an appeal to Germans to accept the legitimacy of the Nuremberg trials and to see them as contributing to the construction of a new and cosmopolitan Europe. Cosmopolitan Europe was consciously created and launched by Jaspers's intervention as the political antithesis to a nationalistic Europe and the physical and moral devastation it had wrought. Jaspers saw cosmopolitan Europe as a reaction to the traumatic experience of the perversion of European values. For him, the Nuremberg court created legal categories and a trial procedure that went far beyond the sovereignty of the nation-state. It did so for practical reasons. It was the only way to capture in legal concepts and court procedures the unprecedented nature of what the Nazis did. Jaspers saw the opportunity to create a new cosmopolitan law of individual responsibility for all perpetrators outside the national legal context and based on the community of nations. For Germans, this meant returning to their own tradition of Kantian Enlightenment but at the same time associating it with a Western model of individual moral responsibility.[2] Legal measures against citizens of one's own state now became crimes against humanity. So if the state was a criminal state—and for Jaspers the distinction between a criminal state and a state that commits crimes is crucial—an individual who served this state could still be charged and sentenced for his misdeeds before an international court of law. This cosmopolitan legal principle was designed to protect civilians not from the violence of other hostile states but from violence committed by their own state—or, more important, against its noncitizens, against people deemed outside its legal boundaries though living within its borders. In many ways, Jaspers's vision reflected the new principles of the human rights regime. Jaspers wanted to identify the postwar era and the Nuremberg trials as the beginning of this new transnational world.

At this juncture Jaspers needed to respond to a question that remains much more complex than it appears at first sight. Who are crimes against humanity committed against? Were these crimes against the Jews, or against humanity? As we move back and forth in this book between universal and particular definitions of the crimes the Nazis committed, so did intellectuals like Jaspers and Arendt grapple with these questions after the war. In fact, crimes connected to historical injustice, even crimes against humanity and genocide, are crimes committed by political groups, by collectives, against other members of groups. Jaspers had to reckon with those in Germany who argued that the idea of a crime against humanity and its accompanying guilt was a legal nullity because humanity was perceived as an empty concept without legal precedent. Others argued that Nazi practices were normal practices of oppression and that the Allies' imposition of guilt was nothing other than victors' justice. Committed Nazis like Martin Heidegger and Carl Schmitt were among the German apologists who tried to normalize German crimes by arguing that these crimes were either normal practices of war or the result of modern technology (see Fine 2000). Jaspers's book was not only directed against those who resented Germany's rapprochement with the West; it was also an attempt to make the aforementioned distinction between criminal states per se and states that commit occasional crimes. For Jaspers, critical thinking meant first of all being able to make distinctions. Unlike his nationalistic critics, Jaspers envisioned Europe in terms of a European tradition of institutionalized self-criticism. In his opinion, this would enable Europe to find its continuity at the very point at which it broke from the past. It would allow Europe to establish future-oriented forms of memory that could be opposed to national founding myths and myths of warfare, thus leading to a universal self-critique of Europe.

In 1946 Jaspers took part in the Geneva Rencontres Internationales, one of the first meetings of European intellectuals after the war. The theme of the conference, the European spirit, was also the title of Jaspers's lecture. His views on a new cosmopolitan Europe were based on humanistic values found not only in Europe but also in China and India, having emerged during what he called "the Axial Age," from 800 to 200 B.C. Jaspers viewed it as a starting point for a new cosmopolitan Europe based on freedom, history, and science. He imagined this age as a usable past for a new Germany and a new Europe, and he drew references from the Bible, antiquity, Homer, and other iconic figures of European civilization (Jaspers 1951, 238). At the same time, Jaspers did not consider America and Russia part of this European civilization (247–48), a theme that seems to unite much recent core-European discourse. For him, Europe was to become a cultural project in which the European values of the Enlightenment could be preserved as well. This would be a new world order based not on one superpower but rather on interdependent states subordinating themselves to core European values. At the same time, it would be a religious Europe, not necessarily a Christian one but a Europe that believed in the transcendence of man, which for Jaspers also entailed a clear-cut sense of good and evil.

Another participant in the Geneva talks, the Hungarian socialist philosopher György Lukács, objected to Jaspers's attempt to claim a universal heritage at the expense of socialism by putting it, at least implicitly, on a par with fascism. Lukács attacked what he perceived as Jaspers's aristocratic and defeatist speech, portraying it as bankrupt individualism (Kapferer 1993). Instead of the Western and European view Jaspers advocated, Lukács suggested an alliance of all progressive and democratic forces in Europe with the Soviet Union, which he saw as the embodiment of European democracy (Benda 1946, 211). The universalism of the West was opposed by the universalism of the East. The parameters of the early cold war, with alternating claims to universalism and its associated divisive narratives in European memory, were thus put into play.

Attempts to universalize the experience of World War II are also evident in postwar legal deliberations regarding Nazi war criminals. The Nuremberg War Crimes Tribunal introduced a set of legal precedents — like crimes against humanity—addressing violations of what had not yet been termed human rights, and elevated the moral responsibility of the citizen, even against the orders of the state.[3] What today appears as normative was at the time a highly charged and contested terrain on which various political and legal forces struggled to impose their vision of justice and international relations (Taylor 1992). The American understanding of the Holocaust, which framed the Nuremberg trials, was originally universalistic: Nazi war crimes were committed against sixty million people, among them six million Jews. The crimes against the Jews took up a tiny percentage of the total Nuremberg indictment, and the Jews themselves remained abstract victims. Even though, or perhaps precisely because, the Holocaust and the fate of the Jews remained a neglected aspect of the Nuremberg trials, it formed the backdrop for its universalistic message. The struggle at Nuremberg was seen as one between civilization and barbarism. Civilization was the victim, Nazi barbarism the perpetrator. The Jews were there, but they stood for "humanity as a whole."[4]

THE POLITICS OF POPULATION TRANSFERS

Another realm that shaped the balance of universal and particular memories of mass atrocities relates to the effective demotion of particular minority rights and their subordination to a vocabulary of universal human rights. In the final analysis, Beneš's views would eventually become the generalized memories of the war during the late 1940s. Most political leaders in the new postwar Europe welcomed population transfers as the "right" solution to the minority problem: "With the fresh memory of the failure of the League's minority system in their minds, the planners of post-war Europe proposed to solve the problem of minorities not by redrawing frontiers nor by attempting another guarantee of minority rights, but rather by eradicating the minorities themselves" (Zayas 1977, 6).

Based on memories of past failures, peace and stability became magical concepts. Fear of chaos dominated the era. Politically speaking, democracy and its preservation were the foremost goals of those who wanted to create a new order in the West. The transfer of minority populations was considered part of this stability-producing system, a precondition rather than a contradiction of democracy. Furthermore, the transfer of minority populations to places where they constituted majorities was considered to be the fulfillment of the international commitment to self-determination (Preece 1998). Population transfers, with a recurrent if illusory demand for their humane implementation, were perceived not as a violation of human rights but, at least in the popular rhetoric of the time, as their prerequisite. Later, in yet another mnemonic twist, the postwar events would be recast as memories of "ethnic cleansing," a neologism that entered public consciousness in the early 1990s through events in the former Yugoslavia. These memories of "ethnic cleansing" dominated the imagery of human rights abuses and gradually reconciled the division between human and minority rights.

During the postwar period, human rights became the answer and the alternative to minority rights. What was remembered when World War II was over was that minorities were suddenly integral parts of organic communities, which had destructive potential as so-called Fifth Columns and traitors. Abstractions like the notion of minorities were turned into Trojan horses of the particular. For the Germans, minority protection meant first of all protection of ethnic Germans outside Germany. In addition, as Mazower (2004) claims, British and American politicians and those involved in the new order wanted human and individual rights to be the new counterforce against the fascist and later Bolshevist states. From this standpoint, human rights were considered the only viable alternative to minority rights. The League of Nations system had ceased to exist by 1948. In this sense the new universalistic order that emerged from World War II imagined an order organized around the notion of human rights without recourse to ethnic or national particularism. The memory of the consequences of that particularism were too painful morally and too unstable politically. But this universalism came with a price. It pushed the continent into waves of population movements, which were thought of as necessary evils to provide peace and stability. All over Europe ethnic and national minorities were moved from one place to another. "At the conclusion of the First World War it was borders that were invented and adjusted, while people on the whole were left in place. After 1945 what happened was rather the opposite: with one major exception [Poland] boundaries stayed broadly intact and people were moved instead" (Judt 2005, 27).

The attitude toward the universalization of equal rights stood in marked contrast to the specific provisions granted to ethnic minority groups between the wars (Schechtman 1951). The UN actually studied the question in detail and had a Sub-Commission on the Prevention of Discrimination and the Protection of Minorities issue a report on the relationship between human rights (or prevention of discrimination) and minority rights. This report was submitted on June 7, 1949, and it was clear from the wording that the UN did not want any further part in the protection of minorities: "Discrimination implies any act or conduct which denies to certain individuals equality of treatment with other individuals because they belong to particular social groups. . . . The protection of minorities, on the other hand, although similarly inspired by the principle of equality of treatment of all peoples, requires positive action: concrete service is rendered to the minority groups. . . . One requires the elimination of any distinction imposed, and the other requires safeguards to preserve certain distinctions voluntarily maintained" (quoted in ibid., 5). Rather than protection of minorities by the world community of nations, the world now had to be protected from them. The political and conceptual space for human rights was created. Much of this memory about the failures to protect people(s) from mass atrocities would inform the core principles of the UN genocide and human rights conventions discussed below.

Tellingly, in 1993 the same UN subcommission published a report outlining the human rights dimension of population transfers, in which it reconciled the two sets of rights: "The Second World War demonstrated the full destructive potential that emerges from population transfers. However, post-war measures, including the promulgation of laws and international agreements, have not averted this continuing phenomenon. Rather, it has remained a common feature of the conduct of war, as well as peace-time policy. There is little doubt that dramatic population movements carry with them commensurate effects on both domestic and international relations of States. Given the volume of historical memory at our disposal, these effects are largely predictable, usually negative, and often a source of global instability and a threat to security."[5] Thus memories of human rights abuses were yet again transposed and seemingly transformed.

Intellectual and political responses as well as emergent cold war constellations circumscribed the actualization of human rights in the post-war period. However, they provide only a partial picture insofar as these

outlooks and policies continued to be predicated on a conventional definition of nation-state sovereignty. At a time when Enlightenment principles
based on sovereign states' protecting the natural rights of their citizens had
collapsed, questions about possible remedies for indifference to the sufferings of others, both inside and outside the borders of the nation, were
not merely academic but were an integral part of the mnemonic fabric and
actual experience of postwar European societies. True, it was precisely the
extremity of the war and mass atrocities that pushed memories of the war
to the margins of societies in reconstruction (Levy and Sznaider 2001).
In spite of, or perhaps because of, the desire to forget, a general and generalized, even decontextualized sensibility toward human rights thrived.
These sensibilities cannot be reduced to instrumental considerations on
the part of policymakers, however, nor can they simply be subjected to the
reasoning of postwar intellectuals; they also need to be connected to the
cosmopolitanization of sentiments we addressed in chapter 3.

In the immediate aftermath of the war, human rights emerged not
only in response to geopolitical imperatives but also as a decontextualized set of memories driven by a mixture of institutional requirements
and cosmopolitan sentiments. It was precisely the abstract nature of
good and evil symbolized by the Holocaust that contributed to the extra-
territorial quality of cosmopolitan memory and the consolidation of
new ethical norms. Their spread into the arena of international politics
is closely related to a new interpretation of cosmopolitanism. In what
follows, we delineate the theoretical and historical sources of this new
cosmopolitanism and expand on its relevance for the politics of human
rights in a global age.

INSTITUTIONAL MEMORIES OF PAST ABUSES:
THE NUREMBERG TRIALS

Memories of the failures of the League of Nations to protect ethnic minorities and the unprecedented genocidal scope of the Holocaust played a
crucial role in the articulation of new international regulatory measures
during the 1940s. A comparison of Article 15 of the Covenant of the League

of Nations and Article 2 of the Charter of the United Nations is a case in point. The League covenant reinforced the sanctity of domestic jurisdiction and the principle of noninterference as standards of international law. The UN charter, based on the Nuremberg precedent, allows interference if a particular action poses a threat to international peace. Interrupted by the emerging cold war, it would take another four decades before the possibility of intervention became a legitimate political weapon.

Legal arguments draw their persuasive power from the fact that they are grounded in precedent, which is why contemporary emphasis on the Nuremberg trials makes up such an important part of our story. Thus it was hardly surprising that the Nazi crimes were initially construed as a war of aggression (an existing legal category) rather than as a crime against humanity (an emerging legal category). The basis for the war crime tribunals in Nuremberg and Tokyo were set down on August 8, 1945, in the London Agreement, which articulated the charter of the International Military Tribunal. It listed a number of crimes that were previously not part of international law, posing new challenges to prevailing assumptions regarding state sovereignty. The tribunal rejected the cog-in-the-system theory, which does not recognize individual action in the system of criminal states. The charter of the International Military Tribunal (IMT) in Nuremberg asserted a new cultural and social paradigm that posited the individual subject with his/her rights and responsibilities. The centerpiece of the Nuremberg trials was article 6 of the London Agreement. Emphasizing "crimes coming within the jurisdiction of the Tribunal for which there shall be individual responsibility," it listed three specific offenses: article 6a introduced the notion of crimes against peace, "namely, planning, preparation, initiation or waging of a war of aggression, or a war in violation of international treaties, agreements or assurances, or participation in a Common Plan or Conspiracy for the accomplishment of any of the foregoing."[6] Article 6b focused on "violations of the laws or customs of war." This category of war crimes had a secure footing in the Hague convention of 1907, while 6a was grounded in the Kellogg-Briand agreement of 1928.

It was the notion of conspiracy and the concept of crimes against humanity specified in article 6c, however, that were intended to provide a legal basis to cope with the atrocities of the Holocaust itself. According to article 6c, crimes against humanity included "murder, extermination, enslavement, deportation, and other inhumane acts committed against any civilian population, before or during the war, or persecutions on political, racial, or religious grounds . . . whether or not in violation of domestic law of the country where perpetrated." Article 6c represented a radical departure from existing international law by recognizing individual responsibility not just in wartime, extending protection to one's own civilian population, granting supremacy to international over domestic law, and internationalizing the persecution of minorities. In this sense, the Nuremberg trials affirmed sovereignty, as crimes against Germany's own citizens could be prosecuted only after Germany started its aggressive war. War was still the major crime. Stressing *mens rea* (criminal intent) essentially implied the criminalization of a certain type of politics—namely, the kind of extreme sovereignty envisioned by Carl Schmitt and others. Furthermore, the assumption of criminal intent also implied individual responsibility, signaling a return to liberal attempts to reconcile the tension between individual rights and state sovereignty. Here the tribunal accepted and reaffirmed the Enlightenment notion of individual agency and morality not subsumed by the state. For Hans Joas (2003), this process, in which human rights violations are treated as criminal acts within states, and through which a relatively autonomous law filled the gap between politics and morality, is one of the most significant consequences of the Nuremberg tribunal. It would have far-reaching consequences for the legal memory of Nuremberg itself, albeit fifty years later, through the ratification of the International Criminal Court, where political accountability and criminal responsibility would be interwoven into one procedure.

THE UNIVERSAL DECLARATION OF HUMAN RIGHTS

Memories of the horrors of the Holocaust also formed the backdrop against which human rights norms and a host of other UN conventions initially established their legitimacy. War atrocities themselves had not previously led to the triumph of human rights. They were not part of international relations prior to World War II: not even the Covenant of the League of Nations contained references to such ideas. In contrast, human rights have a central place in the preamble and Article 1 of the UN charter. The link between the Holocaust and the emergence of a moral consensus about human rights is particularly evident in the genesis and consolidation of the Universal Declaration of Human Rights that was adopted by the General Assembly of the newly formed United Nations on December 10, 1948.

The declaration, as well as the UN charter itself, must be understood as direct responses to the shared moral revulsion of the delegates to the Holocaust—a sentiment that was also reflected in the direct connection between the declaration and some of the legal principles established in the Nuremberg trials. This link was also manifested in the close working relationship between the UN War Crimes Commission and the Human Rights Division of the nascent United Nations (Morsink 1999, 345). In both cases, concerns about the illegality of retroactive jurisprudence were overcome by replacing conventional (i.e., national) legal principles with the broader notion of international law and its implicit appeal to a civilized consciousness, now viewed as a safeguard against the barbarous potential of national sovereignty. Together they were decisive in shaping the way contemporary human rights norms limit state sovereignty by providing international standards for how states can treat their own citizens.

A brief look at the origins of the Universal Declaration of Human Rights is instructive. It was the recent memory of the Holocaust that let "so many delegations from so many different nations and cultural traditions come to an agreement about a universal moral code" (ibid., 36). In his analysis of the various draft stages of the declaration and the debates in which committee members engaged, Johannes Morsink makes a persuasive case that each and every article of the declaration ultimately reflects revulsion at the horrors of the Holocaust. The very notion of these rights grew directly out of what was then considered its worst breach, namely, the crimes of the Nazis. Hence the declaration states in its preamble, "whereas disregard and contempt for human rights have resulted in barbarous acts which have outraged the conscience of

mankind." It was clear to the framers of the declaration which barbarous acts were meant. Human rights are therefore not based on clear-cut
philosophical or religious worldviews but on historical experiences and
concomitant memories of catastrophes.

THE UN GENOCIDE CONVENTION

This mindset was also echoed when the UN declared "genocide" a crime
and asserted that human beings had universal rights. A telling example
of how the Holocaust served as the implicit background for the incipi-
ent implementation of universal values in the late 1940s but was not
explicitly named can be found in the UN genocide convention, which was
adopted by the General Assembly on December 9, 1948. As mentioned
earlier, the term "genocide" was coined in 1944 by Raphael Lemkin, a
Polish Jew. No doubt the example of the Holocaust (a term he did not use)
was the trigger for his efforts to warn the world about systematic attempts
to annihilate specific groups. To his mind, however, genocide was by no
means synonymous with the extermination of the Jews. Instead, Lemkin
justified his efforts with references to genocidal activities that had taken
place before and after the Holocaust. He was eager, as were so many
others, not to present the Holocaust as an exclusive threat for European
Jewry, as is made clear in an essay he published in 1946: "The Nazi leaders had stated very bluntly their intent to wipe out the Poles, the Russians;
to destroy demographically and culturally the French element in Alsace-
Lorraine, the Slavonians in Carniola and Carinthia. They almost achieved
their goal in exterminating the Jews and Gypsies in Europe" (1946, 227).
Accordingly, the Convention on the Prevention and Punishment of the
Crime of Genocide defined genocide in the broadest possible terms as
any of a number of acts "committed with intent to destroy, in whole or in
part, a national, ethnical, racial or religious group."[7] The perceived tension between universalism and particularism also informed liberal critics
of the genocide convention, who objected to the collectivist and somewhat
essentialist bias in its definition of who constitutes the object of genocide.
The convention can be criticized for its nonuniversalistic declaration, in

that only the killing of particular communities is considered genocide. As such, the convention was seen as expressing a deeply illiberal approach (for criticism along these lines, see Holmes 2002). At the same time, this argument goes to the crux of a more cosmopolitan understanding of liberalism and universalism. Yes, the convention expresses concern only for specific groups (recall that the Soviet delegation refused to include the term "political groups" in the text), but does this wording constitute an attack on universalism? This dichotomy echoes historiographical and other debates on the Holocaust: was it a crime against humanity or a crime against the Jewish people? Can it not be both? Is the attack on particular aspects of humanity not an attack on humanness as well? Lemkin certainly thought so (see also Ignatieff 2001a). In such ways, the cosmopolitanized definition of humanity—seen not as a universal concept but as the sum of its particularities—comes to the fore in the convention that aims to prevent genocide. To be sure, this does not mean that the mere presence of a convention has prevented genocidal perpetrators from continuing to act with impunity. But it gives those who want to fight genocide a legal and moral language with which to resist it. Political realism and idealism do not have to contradict each other.

Our approach differs insofar as its focus is neither metaphysical silence nor intellectual despair at the modern project. Instead, we show how human rights abuses have been remembered through institutions and the ritualistic power of criminal trials. These memories, based on shared negative sentiments about the Holocaust and related genocidal iconography, are not only able to produce despair at the modern world but actually help enlightened ideas come to the fore (Rorty 1993). It is a sentiment founded on a universality that is not derived from reason but rather is based on common experiences of human wrongs. "Human wrongs are everywhere; all societies find it easier to recognize and agree upon what constitute wrongs elsewhere than they do rights; wrongs are universal in a way rights are not" (Booth 1999, 62). As such, universal human rights are "a new, welcome fact of the post-Holocaust world" (Rorty 1993, 115). What matters, then, are not the mass atrocities per se, but rather that we now remember atrocities as human rights abuses.

6

THE COLD WAR PERIOD:
MORE THAN ONE UNIVERSALISM

The third period (1949–89) reflects the impact of the cold war on the dissemination of human rights values and vice versa. The conventional story line suggests that the cold war and its ideological divisions interrupted universal interpretations and forestalled a global outlook (Gaddis 2006; Judt 2005). The prospect of a human rights regime essentially went into suspended animation, with the first signs of resurrection coming during the ratification of basic rights documents in the 1970s. On the one hand, ideological divisions precluded the widespread dissemination of human rights protections, while on the other hand, the cold war constituted an important backdrop to both the articulation and the implementation of such protections. To fully grasp the impact of the cold war on the intersection of human rights and sovereignty, it is imperative to differentiate between two historical circumstances. The nascent conditions of the cold war, with its competing visions of universalism in the late 1940s and the politics of fear of the 1950s, were the context for the ideological division and de facto suspension of human rights. By contrast, the beginning of détente between the United States and the Soviet Union placed the issue of human rights in a context that saw the emergence of civil society movements, a growing involvement of nonstate actors, and transnational ties during the 1970s that challenged the primacy of the national sovereign.

THE IDEOLOGICAL SCOPE OF HUMAN RIGHTS

From its inception, the cold war was an obstacle to transforming the human rights declarations of the postwar period into major features of international politics. The fact that the Soviet Union abstained from voting for the Universal Declaration of Human Rights when it was adopted on December 10, 1948, was not a particularly promising start but a predictable one. As mentioned above, the United States and the Soviet Union, the two victors in World War II, represented two different versions of universalism. The former stood for the universalism of individual liberties and a market economy and therefore showed an elective affinity with the basic contours of the human rights regime, while the Soviet system could not accept this regime as emancipatory since it was counterintuitive to its ideology of socialist emancipation. This had institutional and political consequences that turned human rights rhetoric into a weapon of the cold war, one that was no less effective than missiles.

Cold war alliances and the reaffirmation of national sovereignties remained the pillars of international relations, which made the universalistic aspirations of the immediate postwar period as a globally binding ideal largely irrelevant. Nevertheless, the Declaration of Human Rights never vanished, and it became part of competing rights systems, as was evident in the distinction between political and civil rights, on the one hand, and economic, social, and cultural rights, on the other. The West focused on individuals' civil and political rights and blamed the Soviet Union and other Communist states for violating them. Communist and nonaligned states emphasized collective rights, stressing social and economic issues. This division has informed debates on the nature and implementation of human rights protections ever since. As we shall see in our discussion of more recent developments, it is precisely the tension between these two approaches to human rights that defines the ongoing negotiations about the scope of the human rights regime (Beetham 1995; Falk 2000).

The ideological fault lines that shaped the contours of a bipolar world also characterized the debates leading up to the ratification of the UN genocide convention in 1948. While the United States pushed for a broad definition of genocide that would include Stalinist atrocities, the Soviet Union tried to tie the notion of genocide as closely as possible to the extermination policies of the Nazis. As the former ally (USSR) became the prime antagonist, and the former enemy (Germany) an important partner, Nazism and Communism were now viewed as comparable regimes and subsumed under totalitarianism theories. The fact that human rights violations and blatant disregard for many of the norms sustaining them abounded as well explains why the protection of human rights remained stranded in the rhetorical realm of a declaration alone.

The cold war and the accompanying political developments of the era amounted to a politics of fear, and not only the fear that politics could be turned into a mechanism of violence and terror, as exercised by Nazi Germany. During the first two postwar decades it extended beyond the notion of bodily integrity to involve trepidation over nonphysical forms of oppression. Fears of excessive power and the suspension of liberties, the cornerstones of liberal democracies, were projected onto the Soviet Union. The code word for this fear was "totalitarianism" (Gleason 1995). As mentioned earlier, Judith Shklar called this particular political sentiment "the liberalism of fear," which she described as characterized by a political outlook based on memories of what can happen when liberalism is suspended.[1] It was this kind of fear that informed the preamble of the Universal Declaration of Human Rights: "Whereas disregard and contempt for human rights have resulted in barbarous acts which have outraged the conscience of mankind, the advent of a world in which human beings shall enjoy freedom of speech and belief and freedom from fear and want has been proclaimed as the highest aspiration of the common people."

"Freedom from fear" would become the defining feature of the politics of memory during the cold war. It was the memory of what Europe had become, now refracted through the prism of totalitarianism, that informed the new politics of human rights. As Shklar states in her seminal essay, "the freedom it wishes to secure is freedom from the abuse of power and intimidation of the defenseless that difference invites. . . . The liberalism of fear, on the contrary, regards abuses of public powers in all regimes with equal trepidation" (1998, 9). Contrary to the imaginary

Hobbesian notion of the "natural condition of mankind," from which the sovereign leads his subjects into the promised land of political security, Shklar's view of totalitarian regimes is not an intellectual construct but the result of political memory, namely, the memory of Europe before, during, and after World War II. Safeguarding against cruelty as effectively as possible in the future is the universal aim of "liberalism from fear." For Shklar, "systematic fear is the condition that makes freedom impossible" (11). Political memories of totalitarianism are based not on future hopes for a better world but on past memories of a cruel and evil one. One cannot predict the future but only fear the past. The cold war debates on human rights were based not on hope but on memory. Human rights in this respect are first of all based on memories of evil, which are then translated into the hope that such evil will not recur. This is the meaning of the cry "never again" that motivated the human rights regime in that period.

THE SPREAD OF HUMAN RIGHTS: THE HELSINKI EFFECT

Intellectual misgivings must be translated into politics and institutionalization. This was accomplished during the 1960s. The parameters of East-West rivalry affected the formalization of the International Covenant on Economic, Social, and Cultural Rights (ICESCR) and the International Covenant on Political and Civic Rights (ICPCR) during the 1960s. They transformed the UDHR from a purely symbolic resolution into a set of international treaties with mechanisms for monitoring the compliance of the states that ratified them. Despite ideological divisions, these international human rights covenants provided the foundations for the dissemination of human rights.[2] Most of the main human rights treaties were adopted during this period and during the 1980s, that is, before the "official" end of the cold war.[3]

This gradual institutionalization of human rights provisions constituted the backdrop for the subsequent East-West agreement in the 1975 Helsinki accords. Soviet compliance with this effort was predicated on the incorporation of other Helsinki provisions that would ensure territorial integrity and sovereignty. Human rights activists, however, in both the East and the West, gradually created a space for political action outside the state that would adjust the global discourse on human rights to the particular circumstances of Communist regimes (Thomas 2001). What started out as a safeguard for sovereignty would become a central resource for undermining the legitimacy of the sovereign. As Daniel Thomas puts it, the "expansion of civil society under the banner of human rights, the corrosive effects of dissent on the legitimacy and self-confidence of the party-state, and Western governments' insistence on linking diplomatic relations to implementation of human rights norms convinced a growing number of communist elites of the necessity of political (rather than purely economic) reform" (2001, 211). Even if all of these accomplishments cannot be ascribed to Helsinki, there is little doubt that it elevated human rights to another level.

To be sure, this rapid dissemination did not put an end to human rights violations. On the contrary, repressive regimes tended to adopt human rights treaties as window dressing. This discrepancy between words and deeds could be misinterpreted as evidence for the persistence of sovereign impunity and the unfettered pursuit of national interests. Viewed in historical context, however, it is clear that the initial impetus for human rights treaties since the mid-1970s has infringed considerably on the sovereignty of nation-states. Emilie Hafner-Burton and Kiyoteru Tsutsui (2005) speak of a "paradox of empty promises." As nation-states make formal legal commitments to parody human rights compliance even while they are in violation, this process of empty institutional commitment to a weak regime has paradoxically empowered nonstate advocates to pressure governments to move toward compliance.

Seen in this light, Helsinki helped broaden the scope of political action by conferring legitimacy on nonstate actors. Despite the statist stalemate, or possibly precisely as a remedy for it, human rights have increasingly been addressed by NGOs (Boli and Thomas 1997). This expansion must be interpreted in conjunction with the emergence of new social movements in most Western liberal democracies during the 1970s. Thus the human rights agenda did not merely thrive in this climate but greatly contributed to a movement of awareness that transcended the national gaze. Between 1973 and 1985 there was a substantial increase in trans-national human rights NGOs and advocacy networks (Risse, Ropp, and Sikkink 1999).

During the early cold war period, Article 2(7) of the UN charter, pro-hibiting intervention in "matters that are essentially within the domestic jurisdiction of states," remained the decisive operational framework, fre-quently leaving the actual implementation of human rights unenforced. While the political efficacy of human rights was severely circumscribed by ideological splits, supranational bodies such as the UN continued to con-solidate actions during the later cold war period. The UN played an instru-mental role by functioning as an umbrella, allowing intergovernmental organizations (IGOs) to transcend political cleavages and thus justify the aspiration to global justice as a universal project. In short, human rights initiatives proliferated during this period, a trajectory that must be read against two important developments beginning in the 1960s that took on institutional shape in the early 1970s. The first was geopolitical changes and the onset of the East-West détente. The second consisted of the redi-rection of the rights agenda to an increasing number of nonstate actors that reflected the growth of social movement activities in civil society.[4]

Another indicator of the transformation of sovereignty can be seen in the changing relationship between INGOs and IGOs. "INGOs can lead to the formation of IGOs . . . [and] have often been instrumental in helping to shape IGO activities, policies, and agendas." Conversely, "the creation of an IGO institutionalizes the related social sector at the global level; in a world of diffused formal authority, this legitimates the cre-ation of INGOs in that sector" (Boli and Thomas 1999, 29). This trend is apparent in the formalization of relations between IGOs and INGOs and the consultative status many NGOs now enjoy with UN agencies. Since 1996, for instance, the economic and social forum of the UN has officially recognized this consultative status and divides NGOs into cat-egories with different degrees of rights, ranging from mere observers to the entitlement to file petitions and be heard in the General Assembly.

States have not forfeited their sovereignty, but they rely increas-ingly on the standard-setting expertise and lobbying clout that INGOs have cultivated since the early 1970s and honed with the rise of global communication and media technologies. These trends, together with greater democratization of politics in the world, have also contributed to the global spread of NGOs. De-territorialized and relatively inexpensive means of communication have facilitated the emergence of NGOs that once lacked the resources to get their message out. With the formalization of these relationships, a "process through which principled ideas (beliefs about right and wrong held by individuals) become norms (collective expectations about proper behavior for a given identity), which in turn influence the behavior and domestic structure of states," has flourished (Risse, Ropp, and Sikkink 1999, 7). The groundwork for these processes and for the formation of a human rights regime can be attributed to the work of INGOs and IGOs since the mid-1970s.

The success of such a regime, however, is not inevitable but has depended on the end of the cold war and the emergence of globally televised human rights abuses, most notably the Balkan wars of the 1990s and their association with a universalized script of the Holocaust. During the first half of the post–cold war period (until 2001) the human rights regime became formalized, and legitimate sovereignty, both domestic and international, was measured by the extent to which a state could claim adherence to human rights principles. After 2001, changing memories and articulations of fear became a simultaneous source for challenging the human rights regime and opposing the expansion of executive powers, as discussed in the next chapter.

7

THE POST–COLD WAR PERIOD:
GLOBALIZATION AND THE COSMOPOLITAN TURN

States make injustices, and memories of injustices make the state. The championing of human rights has a long history, but a global human rights regime did not come into being until the end of the cold war. The end of ideological alliances determined by a bipolar world signaled a new phase in the formalization of the relationship between human rights NGOs and international agencies, most notably the UN. Without the ideological competition between East and West, which had long hindered the enforcement of human rights policies, there was a general sense that collaboration between NGOs and the UN was a perfect instrument with which to develop effective strategies to improve democratic conditions and prophylactic efforts aimed at preventing genocide and other abuses. Given these expectations, memories of the failure to prevent human rights abuses in the Balkan wars of the 1990s were a driving force behind institutionalizing extensive sets of human rights principles (Levy and Sznaider 2005).

One example of the greater clout of the human rights regime lies in the loss of legitimacy incurred by noncompliance with international human rights laws (Keck and Sikkink 1998). Accusations of human rights abuses can no longer be defended through sovereign rhetoric invoking national interest, nor can they be dismissed as illegitimate meddling in domestic affairs (Wotipka and Tsutsui 2008). Continual transformations of international law practices and the proliferation of war crime trials have consolidated this regime. The juridification of politics has provided the institutional and symbolic context for the ongoing institutionalization of human rights protections and propelled them into a global norm with prescriptive powers. The influence of the human rights regime extends beyond the legal and regulatory features of nations. The cosmopolitan framework presented below overcomes the nation-centric conceptual toolkit that dominates the social sciences to account for these developments.

THE COSMOPOLITANIZATION OF THE HUMAN RIGHTS REGIME

The human rights regime has followed a trajectory marked by a gradual shift from a discourse of universalism from the postwar period and throughout the cold war, which initially imposed itself from the outside and frequently was a matter of external conformity, to a cosmopolitan outlook (since the 1990s) that is developing as an endogenous factor of political rationality rendering human rights politically and culturally consequential. We view the cosmopolitanization of sovereignty as a process marked by historical junctures. We stress the internalization of cosmopolitan principles and the concomitant endogenous reconfiguration of how the state organizes its sovereignty. Notable violations persist, though they create public controversies that serve, on the symbolic level and politically, to confirm the normative strength of human rights protections. Clearly, cosmopolitan rhetoric may still be no more than a smokescreen behind which human rights abuses continue with impunity. One approach is to tally the increasing number of states that have internalized human rights norms and associated them with national principles as the main source of legitimate sovereignty. As we show in detail below, the proliferation of domestic human rights trials during the 1990s and the ratification of the International Criminal Court (ICC), which was established in 2002 as a permanent tribunal to prosecute individuals for human rights violations, are main sources recasting sovereignty.[1]

Our analysis of the post–cold war period focuses on two dimensions in tracing the cosmopolitanization of sovereignty. We first present an account of the universal dissemination of human rights protections and its implications for the emergence of a cosmopolitan idiom. The birth of the human rights regime during the second half of the twentieth century is widely documented (Bonacker 2003; Cole 2005; Donnelly 1999), substantiating that the ratification of human rights treaties confers legitimacy. An analysis of the post–cold war era reveals an internalization of cosmopolitan principles despite contested domestic power constellations. Successful local institutionalization of global norms depends on the way in which they are made congruent with preexisting institutional frameworks through a variety of strategies (Acharya 2004). Accordingly, local conditions of appropriation require greater scrutiny. The cosmopolitanization of sovereignty is a contested process that is contingent on the feasibility conditions of particular historical periods and specific geopolitical constellations.

A central feature of the post–cold war period is the juridification of politics and the fact that norm-generating jurisdiction is frequently driven by nonstate actors who are not tied to any particular nation-state. This was demonstrated in 1993 during the World Conference on Human Rights in Vienna, which attracted 180 states and a large number of nongovernmental participants. It was a significant moment for the future of an emerging human rights regime as well as for a more inclusive human rights agenda that recognized the validity of both political/civic and social/economic/cultural rights (Beetham 1995; Boyle 1995). So-called realists may dismiss these declarations as merely symbolic and normative manifestations.[2] But human rights conventions must be seen as "the end product of international diplomacy, and are a significant means of making sense of the world. [The UDHR] also represents language of commitment which the third force in international human rights politics, after states and international agencies, NGOs, can and will use to effect in all parts of the world on behalf of the victims they exist to represent" (Boyle 1995, 81).

Many of these claims had been voiced earlier, but it was the transformation of state sovereignty as enshrined in Article 2(7) of the UN charter that was decisive. Previously, claims of sovereignty took clear precedence and usually even prevented the UN from responding to complaints by victims of human rights abuses. Whereas during the cold war the refusal to abide by human rights treaties was common practice, the next wave of democratization, during the 1990s, created new pressures. For many democratizing countries, adherence to the ICPCR has become a benchmark of international legitimacy. Two decisions made the Vienna conference a seminal event in the creation of a human rights regime. The first was the appointment of a UN commissioner for human rights, which provided a formal recognition of the regime's significance for international politics and extended its arbitration into the realm of human rights. The other key development is expressed in paragraph 8 of the Vienna declaration, which states that "democracy, development and respect for human rights and fundamental freedoms are interdependent and mutually reinforcing." Acknowledgment of the connection between social/economic and political/civic rights reflects a distinctive post–cold war sensibility. Ratification has proceeded rapidly, albeit unevenly. Clearly one can point to the repeated refusal of some nations to ratify either the political/civil covenant or the economic/social/cultural covenant. However, given the long-standing refusal of the United States to formally recognize these international treaties, despite the fact that it largely initiated them, and given Russia's long-lasting insistence that individuals should not be allowed to lodge complaints against the state, it is remarkable that the United States has recently ratified the ICPCR and the convention against torture, and that Russia now allows its citizens to petition both domestic and international treaty bodies against itself. Changing geopolitical constellations and reactions to a number of humanitarian crises, which are continually addressed with reference to past failures to prevent genocide, have pushed the human rights regime to the forefront of global attention.

THE LIMITS OF UNIVERSALISM: HUMANITARIAN INTERVENTIONISM AND UNIVERSAL JURISDICTION

A visible instance of the transformation of nation-state sovereignty is the use of force to engage in "humanitarian intervention" (Holzgrefe and

Keohane 2003). The standard justification for humanitarian intervention is the allegation that gross violations of human rights are occurring on such a massive scale as to override the foundational principle of the Westphalian order, namely, that territorial sovereignty is inviolate. There are numerous examples, starting with the Congo in 1964, but it was the historical backdrop of the Balkan crisis and memories of unsuccessful demands for intervention in Bosnia, prompting memories of the Holocaust and pressures for intervention in Kosovo, that set new standards.[3]

In contrast to the genocide in Rwanda in 1994, interethnic warfare in Kosovo in 1999, with its European setting and its televised images, resonated strongly with Holocaust iconography. By the late 1990s the Holocaust had been decontextualized as a concept and dislocated from space and time, precisely because it could be used to dramatize any act of injustice. The Holocaust has been turned into a symbol of genocidal holocaust rather than a real historical event. Genocide, ethnic cleansing, and the Holocaust are blurred into an apolitical and ahistorical concept circumscribed by human rights as the positive force and nationalism as the negative. The military and humanitarian intervention in Kosovo was thus framed primarily as a moral obligation largely in response to memories of previous failures to intervene on behalf of innocent civilians. The catchphrase "never again Auschwitz" was frequently invoked, but it was no longer only the failure to stop the Holocaust. The slogan "never again" was simultaneously a reminder of World War II and of the delayed involvement in Bosnia.

This transposition of Holocaust memories onto contemporary sensibilities about genocide propelled the Nuremberg concept of "crimes against humanity" into the global arena. The war in Kosovo is one example of the changed relationship between legal sovereignty and the legitimacy conferred by adherence to a rights discourse. In the absence of a clear UN mandate, the war was technically illegal. Nevertheless, an independent international commission on Kosovo concluded that even in the absence of formal legality, humanitarian intervention was legitimate.[4] As controversial as they continue to be, humanitarian interventions that have long been mooted by no real expectation of response are now considered policy options (Holzgrefe and Keohane 2003).

Humanitarian interventionism has been widely criticized, however, and what looked like a promising extension of a global human rights culture during the late 1990s has since become a highly contentious topic, effectively leading to its suspension. The reasons for this opposition are manifold and range from the (predictable) defense of national sovereignty to arguments that protection of human rights should remain the responsibility of the United Nations. Moreover, the subjective and highly politicized decision-making process leading to humanitarian intervention further contributed to the discrediting of the concept. No less important, and in tune with our overall argument, is the underlying claim to universalism that has mobilized resistance. Weak (and often non-Western) states have complained about the asymmetry of the practice—i.e., that it enables strong states to interfere in their sovereign affairs. Some have dismissed the universalistic claims attached to humanitarian interventionism as a form of neocolonialism (Chomsky 1999). Still others have suggested that imposing the Western ideal of liberal democracy is dismissive of particular local cultures (Žižek 2005). Our point is not to adjudicate these ongoing disputes but to acknowledge that here, too, we recognize an overbearing universalism that does not sufficiently account for a certain degree of particularism; that is, a position that privileges ethnic, cultural, or national principles ultimately is perceived as undermining the power of the human rights regime.

Another indication of the political limits of universalism was the early demise of the concept of universal jurisdiction. The basic idea behind this principle was that a state can exercise jurisdiction over criminal deeds that were not committed on its territory irrespective of the nationality of the perpetrator or any relation whatsoever with the country that seeks to prosecute the violations. Universal jurisdiction would thus be justified, for instance, when the crime is one against humanity, under the same kind of *jus cogens* that has informed international war crime trials since Nuremberg. The concept received widespread attention when Belgium's "law of universal jurisdiction" was legislated in 1993. It has since been applied in several cases, and controversies over its legal relevance and political legitimacy abound.

The influence of global processes in changing the policies of both governments and courts of law can be seen in a series of dramatic events in the international legal arena at the end of the 1990s. These events established transnational prosecutions of human rights violations as a viable alternative, or at least as a complementary strategy, to national and international trials. As a result, states have been pressed to prosecute violators of human rights more heavily than ever before, as a way to uphold their international legitimacy and defend their sovereignty. The actions of the Spanish judge Baltasar Garzón illustrate the growing presence of the Nuremberg ethos and its underlying principle of universality (Roht-Arriaza 2005). In 1996 Garzón demanded the arrest of Argentina's former military dictators for their role in 320 unsolved murders and disappearances of Spanish citizens during the so-called Dirty War. Attracting even wider attention was Garzón's 1998 order of detention against Augusto Pinochet, who at the time was in London. Garzón argued that these were crimes against humanity and thus gave Spain the right to try the offenders under international law. Garzón's attempts to prosecute gross human rights violations across borders established a precedent against heads of state, who may be tried for crimes like torture and genocide, which are no longer considered covered by sovereign immunity. Although Pinochet was eventually found unfit for trial, his arrest and the rash of other transnational prosecutions that followed made a remarkable impact on the perception of transnational prosecutions and, as a result, on national ones as well (Roht-Arriaza 2005; Nash 2007). Even though universal jurisdiction has limited actual appeal, it carries great symbolic weight, for it reaffirms both a de-territorialized definition of sovereignty and notions of individual responsibility. Furthermore, it embeds particular and at times biased or willfully construed historical memories of past abuses into a global narrative of human rights imperatives.

In institutional and political terms, however, the notion of universal jurisdiction has in fact been a temporary phenomenon with limited political salience. Faced with a multitude of formal requests to prosecute political leaders of both dictatorships and democratic countries for war crimes, Belgium eventually amended its 1993 law of universal jurisdiction in 2003, significantly restricting the scope of its reach and effectively rendering it meaningless. Another institutional limitation essentially superseding the universality principle was the creation of the International Criminal Court in 2002.

Ultimately, the concept of universal jurisdiction has limited appeal because its underlying legal rationale operates within a universalistic framework that does not sufficiently consider local and national circumstances and even seeks to circumvent them. This limitation has both formal and informal dimensions. It has been criticized for the democratic deficit that it entails, since courts administering universal jurisdiction are essentially unaccountable to the citizens of the nation they seek to prosecute. Despite the general consensus that justice can be global in scope and the widespread symbolic appeal of universal jurisdiction, its lack of incorporation of local conditions ultimately prevented it from turning moral perceptions into soft law.

During the 1990s the inviolability of the nation-state was tested through humanitarian interventions and public debates about the value of universal jurisdiction. Both practices were predicated on a strong universalism and proved to be controversial. They ultimately led to the renewed affirmation of the legal and regulatory features of the state, which supports our argument that the normative power of the human rights regime extends beyond exogenous pressures. Rather than undermining sovereignty itself, the institutionalized mediation of universalistic and particularistic (i.e., national) principles poses a threat to the primacy of nationhood as the guiding principle of political legitimacy. Ultimately, sovereignty is recast in terms of domestic legal measures that are subsumed under juridical procedures emphasizing legal complementarity. The interactive process through which sovereignty is gradually denationalized is the focus of the remainder of this chapter.

FROM INTERNATIONAL TO HYBRID AND DOMESTIC WAR CRIME TRIALS

The cosmopolitanization of sovereignty is reflected not only in the high adoption rate of human rights treaties but in different (local) modes of incorporation, as evidenced by the dramatic rise in domestic war crime trials in the past two decades. The power of the human rights regime since the 1990s consists of the incorporation of international law into domestic jurisdictions by way of localization. This cultivation of domestic courts is not an aberration but in many ways is the result of changes in international law. The strongest manifestation of the cosmopolitanization of sovereignty can be seen in the proliferation of specific types of human rights trials. These include *international trials* (e.g., Yugoslavia, Rwanda), *hybrid trials* that combine international and national features (e.g., Cambodia), and finally, a strong recent trend toward *domestic trials* (e.g., Argentina), characterized by national prosecution of human rights violators, based largely on the incorporation of international law. The proliferation of domestic trials and the ratification of the International Criminal Court as a main instrument in reinforcing sovereignty point to the strong cosmopolitan interplay of local and global dynamics.

THE UNIVERSALIST ETHOS OF THE NUREMBERG TRIBUNAL

Initially, the universalistic approach was reinforced through the legal inscription of the Nuremberg ethos. In February 1993 the UN Security Council demanded the establishment of an "International Tribunal to Prosecute Persons Responsible for Humanitarian Law Violations in Former Yugoslavia" (ICTY). It started its work in 1994. Nuremberg was the undisputed legal and moral precedent for this tribunal, which was the first such body created since the end of World War II. As in Nuremberg, the trial's task was not to write history but to establish juridical responsibility. As in Nuremberg, however, the history of the massacre in Srebrenica and other war-related events was in fact written in this trial. The ICTY was an outright challenge to sovereignty. A similar dynamic was also apparent in the UN war crimes tribunal for Rwanda. Here, too, memories of the universal message of generalized responsibility of Nuremberg hovered over the trial. The prosecution, for instance, referred to Nuremberg explicitly when the tribunal accused three men of inciting Rwandan Hutus to murder Tutsis and moderate Hutus. "It is the first time since Julius Streicher, the Nazi publisher of the anti-Semitic weekly *Der Stürmer*, appeared before the Nuremberg judges in 1946 that a group of journalists stands accused before an international tribunal on such grave charges," the *New York Times* reported. "Prosecutors have drawn stark parallels between the vitriolic campaigns against the Jews by *Der Stürmer* before World War II and the actions of some Rwandan media organizations before and during the 1994 slaughter of the Tutsi" (Simons 2002, 3).

These international trials are important symbolic events that have attracted a great deal of global media attention because they signal the centrality of human rights in international and domestic politics. They have also received a great deal of criticism, however, both from politicians with vested interests and, even more so, from legal scholars concerned with the integrity of international law and its human rights extensions. The former have frequently leveled charges of victor's justice against international trials and have used this criticism to mobilize nationalistic sentiment. The legal community, both in the international and in the domestic realms affected by litigation against human rights abuses in their respective countries, has also been eager to protect its legitimacy and professional autonomy. As a result, more attention has been paid to domestic sensibilities and how they converge or clash with international standards.

THE INTERNATIONAL CRIMINAL COURT

Many of these changes found their expression in the establishment of the International Criminal Court in 2002. On a purely symbolic level the ICC is a global reminder that the shield of sovereign impunity no longer exists. In practice, however, the ICC as the standard-bearer of international law does not undermine sovereignty but effectively reinforces domestic jurisdiction.[5] Sovereignty has been denationalized but also strengthened. The ICC is the result of a long debate about whether cases involving human rights crimes should be prosecuted domestically or internationally. Contrary to the stipulations of the international criminal tribunals, the ICC favors domestic proceedings, provided they meet certain criteria. Complementarity is the key concept in this cosmopolitanization of legal procedures that merge domestic jurisdiction with international standards. Complementarity stipulates the conditions under which the ICC should defer to domestic jurisdiction, and clearly states that the ICC can assume authority only when a state is unwilling or unable to prosecute. Complementarity indicates the legitimacy that states confer on a global institution such as the ICC while at the same time recognizing that these global norms should be part of their domestic jurisdiction. The principle of complementarity "has already prompted national authorities to pass implementing legislation and create judicial structures to deal with international crimes domestically" (Turner 2006, 990). Complementarity thus serves as a cosmopolitanizing mechanism, as it "represents the express will of States Parties to create an institution that is global in scope while recognizing the primary responsibility of States themselves to exercise criminal jurisdiction" (1003). The ICC is a self-reflexive manifestation of the transformations discussed in this book. It represents international recognition that circumscribes state sovereignty in several forms. Like the UN charter, it ensures that statehood remains the central political unit in international law. At the same time, however, it consolidates a hierarchy of values in which human rights supersede the previous untouchable status of nation-state sovereignty. Article 7 in particular, dealing with "crimes against humanity," solidifies this shift, for it blurs the distinction between international and internal conflicts. Paradoxically, the dissemination of human rights norms and the success of the ICC can be measured in terms of the limited number of cases before the ICC.[6] That is, most states confronted with the possibility of losing a case at the ICC are inclined to comply with the requirements for domestic prosecution. Here again there is a trajectory that starts out with concerns about loss of legitimacy, then involves a gradual institutionalization of global norms, and finally achieves their voluntary incorporation by merging domestic and international jurisdiction.

The cosmopolitanization of sovereignty is not confined to the ICC and the formal principle of complementarity in the legal and political realms but is also substantiated in trends that show how humanitarian law is increasingly being incorporated into domestic judicial structures (Harland 2000). Domestic courts are frequently called upon to determine whether government actions comply with international human rights norms. Scholars have highlighted the socializing effect of international law on the judicial and political fields (Koh 1997; Fourcade and Savelsberg 2006). The formal adoption of these laws and their significance for domestic jurisdiction are also reflected in the increasing trend toward domestic trials. Sikkink and Walling (2006) address this development in terms of what they call a justice cascade. Their main finding indicates that since the mid-1980s the number of domestic trials increasingly outnumbers hybrid and international trials.

The transformation of sovereignty is thus not leading to the erosion of the state but rather has become a necessary condition for maintaining its legitimacy in the first place. This cosmopolitanized sovereignty blurs conventional divisions between endogenous and exogenous factors. The bonds enabling state, nation, and legitimacy to remain interchangeable, and those that allow authority structures to continue to be perceived as coterminous with geographical entities, have been severed. Despite the strong universalistic underpinnings of the dissemination of human rights norms, it would be misleading to treat cosmopolitanism as synonymous with universalism. Clearly cosmopolitanism seeks validation by adhering to universalistic features. But our empirical analysis confirms that while universalization of legal principles might be a prerequisite for their spread, the salience of cosmopolitan law and its impact on sovereignty is, in the final analysis, a question of how it is being appropriated and localized (Gordon and Berkovitch 2007; Halliday and Carruthers 2007; König 2008). Put differently, what are the tractable conditions in a state, given its current political situation and its legal traditions?

In conclusion, our analysis of the two post–cold war decades demonstrates how the historically contingent link between statehood and nationhood has been severed through the local articulation of nation-transforming human rights norms. The transformative impact of human rights norms on an increasingly denationalized mode of sovereignty is the consequence not only of exogenous pressures but also of how global scripts are locally inscribed. This does not imply a weakening of state sovereignty. On the contrary, the centrality of human rights norms has become a prerequisite for maintaining the legitimacy of a state. We refer to this manifestation of political rationality as the cosmopolitanization of sovereignty.

Our analysis thus reveals a paradox: the nation is being remembered in order to overcome the sovereignty which sustains it. Conflicts between groups and the ongoing tensions between global orientations and particular attachments are invoked in order to reconcile them. Cosmopolitan forms of memory, newly emerging institutions of transnational jurisdiction, negotiations about restitution, and the political relevance of universal human rights are all constitutive elements for these developments. But this cosmopolitanization is neither uniform nor inevitable, let alone consensual. As we have indicated, it is largely driven by conflicts between the local and the global. The process-oriented notion of cosmopolitanization must be understood as a relational concept, pointing to dynamics in which connections between cosmopolitan changes and movements, on the one hand, and resistances and blockades triggered by them, on the other, are analyzed together in their interactive relationships. We turn now to the manifestations (and implications) generated by the persistent antagonism between universal human rights norms and the memories of particular groups. The politics of forgiveness is one realm in which tensions come to the fore between expectations of what is to be remembered and who is remembering what.

HUMAN RIGHTS AND THE CLASH OF MEMORIES:
THE POLITICS OF FORGIVENESS

One of the arenas in which the tensions between the universal and particular meet is that of political forgiveness. Forgiveness in this context
means a new beginning, a capacity not to be determined by the past. This
has become part of a universal norm in which the forgiver and the forgiven are expected to reconcile past evils for the sake of a shared future.
We encounter a dilemma when forgiveness on the personal level and forgiveness on the collective level are fused in a human rights rhetoric commanding reconciliation. With the passage of time, important distinctions
between the memories of perpetrators and victims fade. Memories are
passed on to observers and transmitted through media channels that are
shaped by human rights tropes. In the cosmopolitan context of the new
human rights regime, a compromise is achieved that, however fragile, is
sustained by the mutual recognition of the history of the "Other." This
fusing of perspectives makes the act of reconciliation a key experience of
memory. It is not so much the original crimes that are on the agenda—
the passage of time removes the actual victims and perpetrators, and they
are no longer the actors—rather, it is how their descendants deal with
these histories and memories (Hirsch 2008). In other words, the inclusion of the Other tends to erase the distinction between the memories
of perpetrators and victims. What remains is the memory of a common
history that cannot be divided. The cosmopolitan memory of the past

emerges from the conscious and intended inclusion of the suffering of the Other, and not from the idea of some community of fate, inspired by mythical delusions or the certainty of historical continuity.

Another important ramification of the politics of forgiveness, and possibly even a prerequisite for the potential of reconciliation, that emerges from the temporal and experiential distance is thus a fundamental shift of epistemological viewpoint from one centered on the victim/perpetrator relationship to one focused on the failure of the witness, i.e., the passive bystander. But the passage of time and the global imperative associated with the cultural admonition to bear witness to past injustices from a human rights perspective rather than the epistemological vantage point of victim or perpetrator are not evenly distributed. As discussed in the next chapter, the experience of the (European) West, despite or perhaps precisely because of its global exposure, cannot be generalized and projected onto other regions. Accordingly, a cosmopolitan approach to memory and human rights needs to take into account the fact that local experiences are marked by noncontemporaneities.

Political forgiveness and human rights share a common assumption of absoluteness and sanctity. They also share a break with the past, a new beginning (on this topic, see in particular Arendt 1958). The act of forgiveness refers to joint acts of exercising freedom by breaking loose from the past. The Universal Declaration of Human Rights was predicated on the vision that a new world can be created out of the ashes, that redemption and a new beginning can follow catastrophe. This is not only politics; it is also political theology and political salvation. Forgiveness works in similar ways in that it presupposes a new beginning and salvages the past through new beginnings. Both human rights and political forgiveness are charismatic (Brudholm and Cushman 2009). This is also why debates on forgiveness start from the unchallenged assumption that forgiveness is a morally superior act and the spirit of forgiveness a morally superior sentiment (Digeser 2001). Resentment—the refusal to forgive—is considered atavistic and archaic and supposedly leads to revenge and renewed cycles of violence (Brudholm 2008). It is the equivalent of being against human rights. By contrast, uttering the truth about historical injustices and making this gesture together with the former enemy is considered liberating. Truth commissions in particular are said to have these redemptive qualities, and as such are part of other reconciliatory acts. In this sense, history and politics have been turned into trauma laboratories that probe whether forgiveness, given state-sponsored mass atrocities and other extreme human rights abuses, can be granted in meaningful ways, both personally and collectively (Levy and Sznaider 2006a). There may be no way of determining what constitutes the correct relationship between memories and forgetting, or between punishment, revenge, and forgiveness. But as a framework of global normative expectations, the politics of forgiveness not only dominates contexts of transitional justice and other cases of conflict resolution but also shuns those who do not want to forgive, who demand and insist on their right to resentment and retribution.

The literature on forgiveness, regret, apology, and so on has by now become a specialized field of its own, fusing moral and normative arguments (Barkan and Karn 2006). Sociological thinking counters the belief that politics should be guided by theoretical doctrine, universal principles, or appeals to abstract rights. Sociology can provide an analysis of religion, but it does not consider itself religious. There is a sociology of the metaphysical but no metaphysical sociology. However, as we pointed out in chapter 1, it is precisely this metaphysical zeal that lies at the heart of the contemporary project of global justice and human rights (see also Turner 2009). These facets can best be clarified by analyzing the politico-theoretical thought found in various works by Hannah Arendt, for whom human rights and political forgiveness were linked in her account of the modern predicament of the political subject. Drawing on Arendt, we contend that the political significance of forgiveness is contingent upon a set of historical and institutional circumstances that condition the respective meanings forgiveness can or cannot assume. We briefly examine state-sanctioned restitution measures in that they highlight the ambiguous potential of forgiveness, and we show how the impact of forgiveness depends on the political and moral context in which it is undertaken.

Forgiveness constitutes the implied and often explicit background for issues of restitution, the politics of memory, and other reactions to the public outing of historical injustices. It confronts us with difficult questions. Should we privilege memory over forgetting, punishment over amnesty, resentment over forgiveness? Or, to return to Judith Shklar's metaphor, should we favor the party of hope or the party of memory? Should forgiveness privilege former victims or absolve the perpetrators? These and other questions triggered a rich literature in the aftermath of the Holocaust. Global awareness emerged in the context of postapartheid South Africa with the seminal influence of the Truth and Reconciliation Commission. It received renewed attention against the global backdrop of the Balkan conflicts during the 1990s and regional manifestations of transitional justice such as the Argentinean Dirty War and other Latin American cases, as well in eastern and central European post-Communist societies (Minow 1998; Cushman and Meštrović 1996).

There are different perceptions of forgiveness, but all presume to have the alleged power to undo what has been done, that is, "the possible redemption from the predicament of irreversibility" as Hannah Arendt so aptly put it in the late 1950s (Arendt 1958, 236). It implies freedom of political action, the ability to liberate oneself from the prison of time, to be born anew in politics. As Arendt observes, the opposite of forgiveness is vengeance, and vengeance can be predicted, since it runs its due course in which people act as they are supposed to act, and the past determines the present and the future. Forgiveness, on the other hand, is unpredictable, it is undetermined action; hence, in Arendtian terms, it is true political action and an expression of political liberty (236ff.). The alternative is punishment and trials, and Arendt briefly explores this avenue when she writes that "men are unable to forgive what they cannot punish and they are unable to punish what has turned out to be unforgivable" (241). Arendt claims that such offenses can be neither punished nor forgiven and that they lie outside human control. This view has been somewhat modified with respect to crimes against humanity, where the unforgivable at times is precisely what seeks to be forgiven and juridified.

This is the crux of the problem of the right combination of what Max Weber, who struggled constantly between charisma and routinization in his sociological theories (see Radkau 2009), called *Verantwortungsethik* (ethics of responsibility) and *Gesinnungsethik* (ethics of ultimate ends).

This distinction originated in a famous lecture Weber gave in 1918 entitled "Politics as a Vocation" (Weber 1919/1958). Forgiveness might actually be a bridge between the sacred and the profane (ultimate ends and responsibility), and as such it has the potential to counter Arendt's dictum of irreversibility. We do not want to be prisoners of the past, because only our radical openness to the future makes political action possible. Political forgiveness is thus one possible form of leverage. Arendt recognized the charismatic origins of forgiveness in salvation but reevaluated it in such a way that forgiveness was to be based not on Christian love but on Greek respect. In this way she attempted theoretically to void the concept of its religious content and replace it with a political one. This also links her view of forgiveness with a burgeoning literature that emphasizes the notion of recognition (Somers and Roberts 2008). Her reasoning was highly political without being religious or inwardly oriented. Arendt did not deal with how people feel in the political process. She considered the political world a common space created by people and was less concerned with people's sentiments in the process. This is an important point, as many debates regarding political forgiveness are framed around the notion of whether people employing tropes of forgiveness or apology really mean it.

This charge is also frequently leveled against the political rationale underlying the human rights regime. Critics like Chomsky often suspect ulterior motives and lose sight of the actual remedies human rights politics can promote (see Isaac 2002 on the comparison between Chomsky and Arendt on this point). But more than the human rights regime is at stake here. Debates over *Wiedergutmachung* (restitution), the monetary compensation the Federal Republic of Germany provided to Israel and the Jewish people (see below), are a good example of the way intentions and actual consequences do not always jibe. Restitution is based on a simple notion of justice: people who were deprived of their rights and property should be compensated. According to Arendt, it is the moral equality between forgiver and the forgiven that matters; it is the sharing of a common world between two sides who voluntarily agree to break out of their prisons of the past (Arendt 1958; see also Digeser 2001).

Arendt qualified her view of forgiveness, however, by linking it to the judicial and the political. Deeds that are not punishable cannot be forgiven. What she called "radical evil," Arendt's term for the Holocaust, is thus excluded from the politics of forgiveness. Perpetrator and victim need to share common ground, to be "at home in the world," as she put it. This plurality makes politics possible. Radical evil destroys plurality and therefore politics, because former victims and perpetrators have ceased to share the same world. Following Arendt's line of thought thus poses a huge conceptual problem for theorists and activists of reconciliation and, by extension, for human rights. A human rights regime presupposes that people will submit to it, and this includes perpetrators as well as victims.

What has pushed forgiveness to the forefront of public and political attention? The answer is Christian morality, or rather its secular embodiments such as universalism, which have elevated forgiveness to the status of a supreme, even constitutive value (for a deployment of this argument, see Heyd 2001). Not only does Christianity emphasize internal transformative capacities; it puts suffering and its redemption at the core. The cultural code of Christianity has also been disseminated through processes of cultural globalization (Meyer 1989). But forgiveness as a cultural code does not need its Christian roots. As Arendt writes, "The fact that he [Jesus of Nazareth] made this discovery [of forgiveness] in a religious context and articulated it in religious language is no reason to take it any less seriously in a strictly secular sense" (1958, 238). This is especially true in a global era where accelerated processes of universalization are at the same time processes of secularized Christianity, which can be disseminated across its religious boundaries.

This is abundantly clear in Arendt's criticism of Karl Jaspers's conception of guilt, discussed earlier. Jaspers made a crucial distinction between criminal, political, moral, and metaphysical guilt. The issue of moral guilt is problematic because it presupposes that individuals subordinate their conscience to the demands of the state (Rabinbach 2001). Guilt becomes privatized. This turns guilt into a matter of the soul and not of the courtroom, which in turn cries out for forgiveness and not punishment by law. Placing moral and metaphysical guilt outside the sphere of legal punishment individualizes crimes that were committed collectively. This poses almost insurmountable problems for reconciliation. Locating moral guilt somewhere beyond judicial control shifts it into the realm of memory, a dark shadow lying on the conscience of the former perpetrators—at least in the optimistic outlook of Jaspers in the immediate aftermath of the German defeat in 1945, an outlook he soon abandoned. Jaspers rejected the concept of collective guilt, and his attempts to define different notions of guilt individualized and human-ized the problem. But crimes connected to historical injustice, even genocide and other crimes against humanity, are committed by politi-cal groups, by collectives against other members of groups. The ques-tion remains open whether guilt serves to extirpate responsibility. Since the 1970s Germany's official public culture has sought to distinguish between guilt and responsibility by refusing the collective nature of guilt and insisting on its collective responsibility. As mentioned above, Arendt was aware of this problem as early as 1945 (Fine 2000). According to Arendt, the difficulty was amplified in Germany because it was impos-sible to distinguish between a secret hero and a mass murderer (Arendt 1994, 125). However, Arendt enlarged the problem beyond its German borders: "For many years now we have met Germans who declare that they are ashamed of being Germans. I have often felt tempted to answer that I am ashamed of being human" (131). She accepted Jaspers's notion of moral and metaphysical guilt but wanted to politicize it. In closing her essay she observed presciently that "the idea of humanity, when purged of all sentimentality, has the very serious consequence that in one form or another, men must assume responsibility for all crimes committed by men and that all nations share the onus of evil committed by all others" (131). It is only a short step from this insight to the concept of crimes against humanity.

RESENTMENT AND RETRIBUTION: ANTIDOTES OF FORGIVENESS

Two arguments that reject forgiveness and reconciliation shed light on the tension between global normative expectations and the validation of particular experiences. These arguments are important cries in the wil-derness against attempts at universalization. They attempt to guarantee that local concerns are not completely overwritten by universalistic norms. Expressions of national atonement, fiscal compensation, and other forms of redemption do not necessarily imply forgiveness (for a detailed criticism of political forgiveness as a measure of justice, see Brudholm 2008). Jean Améry and Vladimir Jankélévitch both refuse forgiveness and insist on the moral worth and virtue of resentment. They argue that the passage of time should be resisted, and they deny time the power of moral and legal absolution. They ask for retribution, not forgiveness. They point out that personally forgiving the people who murdered your family or subjected you to inhumane torture is a rare and heroic act that should not be expected of anyone. Améry's and Jankélévitch's refusal to forgive is situated completely within an individual perspective—it is about feelings. It has nothing to do with politics, because no punishment could possibly be enough. If all punishment is meaningless and therefore all reconciliation is meaningless as well, there is only the feeling of resentment and the memory it continues to nurture. The best that can be achieved ins these circumstances is legal justice, although both writers are very much aware that justice can no longer be rendered.

Jankélévitch wrote his essay in the midst of the French debate on the imprescriptability of Nazi crimes. For him, pardon was equal to forgetting. His view was that crimes against Jews are truly crimes against humanity, against the human essence; thus they cannot be pardoned. He also did not believe in German repentance: "German repentance, its name is Stalingrad . . . its name is defeat" (1996, 566). For these reasons, forgiveness may have nothing to do with reconciliation in the sense in which we use the term today, which is set in a social and political perspective independent of personal feelings. No one expects victims to forgive anyone, but the social process of receiving restitution and processes of political forgiveness can still legitimately be considered part of a reconciliation process.

Améry and Jankélévitch, however, seem to be lonely voices in a global trend toward forgiveness and reconciliation. They held on to their resentment and their inability to come to terms with the past: "Today when the Sophists recommend forgetfulness, we will forcefully mark our mute

THE CLASH OF MEMORIES   111

and impotent horror before the dogs of hate; we will think hard about the agony of the deportees without sepulchers and of the little children who did not come back. Because this agony will last until the end of the world" (Jankélévitch 1996, 572). These voices represent resistance to an attitude defined by Jeffrie Murphy, a philosopher of forgiveness, that involves "the overcoming, on moral grounds, of the feeling of resentment . . . and it is particularly important in allowing human relations to continue that otherwise would be disrupted by resentment" (1988, 20). Archbishop Desmond Tutu echoed this view of forgiveness as a civic sacrament that formed the basis for the South African Truth and Reconciliation Commission.

Jacques Derrida's *On Cosmopolitanism and Forgiveness* (2001) addresses similar problems, but Derrida places forgiveness outside the realm of politics: "forgiveness forgives only the unforgivable" (32). Derrida argues for unconditional forgiveness, which forgives the guilty as guilty irrespective of demands for forgiveness and without transforming the guilty into the innocent. Derrida is thus seemingly oblivious to the difference between legal guilt and moral responsibility. This is what Thane Rosenbaum (2003) writes in an article dealing with German attempts to memorialize the Holocaust: "Guilt is a legal term; responsibility is a moral one. Acknowledgment, truth and apologies are moral imperatives; forgiveness is not, precisely because it suggests starting over with a clean slate, which, in this case, only the ghosts are empowered to grant."

However, Derrida does not view forgiveness as a system of exchange. It has nothing to do with reconciliation, and he rejects Jankélévitch's point that "forgiveness died in the camps." Derrida may be attempting to restore radical evil to dimensions where forgiveness is possible, but this implies the impossible—namely, the reconciliation of the universal and the particular, the public and the private. It is salvation translated into politics. Nevertheless, if forgiveness lies outside political action, what does it achieve? Is forgiveness a deconstructive or even a messianic game? In Derrida's world, we base ourselves on some transcendent human substance that needs to be saved, "a dream for thought" (Derrida 2001, 60). In this sense Derrida politicizes the Christian roots of forgiveness to a greater extent than even Arendt. Derrida challenges Arendt's strict political separation between private sentiments and public action by abolishing the line between the private and the public spheres. Thus private and public forgiveness become one and the same.

Furthermore, Derrida's argument begs the question of what we are trying to nurture and preserve. If we are now dealing with subjects without history and context, who even lack identity and obligations to their respective community, what is it that institutionalized justice is set up to protect? What are the guarantees for not being tortured and killed? The abolition of the distinction between the private and the public does away with the demarcation between the particular and the universal as well, because humanity and particular human groups are collapsed into the same conceptual framework.

This raises the classic modernist question of which type of forgiveness can be held accountable. The question revolves around notions of individuality and collectivity and thus is about modern politics. Political forgiveness acknowledges that all are equal and therefore share a common sense of humanity. This seems to be the unconditionality that even the metaphysical Derrida was talking about. The transcendental or even the religious part of our human existence explains why, according to Derrida, forgiveness is Abrahamic, since it is connected to the notion of one God, which makes the human possible. Thus the concept of crimes against humanity is basically a religious or sacred conception in which, as Derrida puts it, "we accuse ourselves of crimes against ourselves"— but it lacks the dimension of the sacred because humanity cannot be the subject of crimes; only a specific group of people can which again makes it conditional. Nevertheless, beside the principle that all men are equal and share a common sense of humanity is another principle that views every individual as unique and irreplaceable. This is the starting point for reconciling the two principles, which connects them through an ethics of responsibility. Although these principles seem logically exclusive, they help us to close in on the limits of universal forgiveness. This is the mechanism linking the sacred and the political, which, we argue, is carried through memory.

Like the tension between the sacred and the political, the discord between individuality and collectivity is also mirrored in the emerging legislative language of international law, especially when it comes to crimes against humanity (Levy and Sznaider 2006a). Victims of genocide and other atrocities lose their individual autonomy when they are targeted because of their group rather than their individual characteristics. Ironically, their subsequent attempts to redeem their individuality also involve a collective approach (i.e., class action suits, which emphasize the collective and categorical). This in turn leads to the recognition of the individual and the abstraction of the crimes and the ensuing processes. This legal conundrum is so problematic because it leads to such questions as how judicial procedures can deal with questions like humanity and crimes against it. This concern was echoed in many of Arendt's deliberations.

It also leaves open the precise nature of the transition from forgiveness to restitution. Legislation and profanation indicate such a shift. This transition may start with forgiveness and end up with restitution, possibly leaving the alleged paradox between individual autonomy and moral conscience intact insofar as the act of forgiveness becomes secondary. In effect, the victim forgives, while restitution is provided by the perpetrator. This is the translation from the metaphysical level to the mundane, and it is how forgiveness is translated into money. It can be argued that in crimes against humanity the event may be beyond understanding, beyond witnessing something only the dead can comprehend, as are the attendant limits of representation. Derrida treats crimes against humanity as crimes we commit against ourselves, meaning that we are all responsible. Thus the crimes and the victims are individualized; the victims are "humanity" rather than, for instance, Jews. The relationship between testimony and representation is mutually constitutive. Questions of truth or authenticity are secondary, especially since the impact of representation on re-created memory and testimony in no way implies that they are untrue.

Ultimately, however, the various constraints and gestures that forgiveness imposes on both collective and individual practices cannot be determined in a metaphysical vacuum but are shaped by historical circumstances and how they are collectively remembered. Here, the Holocaust in particular posed a challenge to the universal Enlightenment premises of reason and rationality: how do we define the reason and rationality of human rights? Paradoxically, the Holocaust functioned simultaneously as the source of a critique of Western universalism and the foundation for a cosmopolitan desire to propagate human rights universally. As we have said, the central question here is whether the Holocaust is part of modernity or the opposite, a return to barbarism that represents the breakdown of modernity, a question that is directly related to the broader debate about whether barbarism constitutes the breakdown of civilization or is very much part of modern civilization, with its thoroughgoing rationalization and bureaucratization. In the same manner it is worth inquiring whether the human rights regime represents a departure from barbarism, a civilizing force, or just another sophisticated form of Western oppression, as critics like Chomsky would have it. As we have seen, there is a good argument to be made that barbarism is an immanent quality of modernity, not its corruption (Horkheimer and Adorno 1944/1972). In this view, civilization ruptures, at least potentially, as a result of the rationalization and bureaucratization that characterize modernity. This approach has become widely popularized in the works of Zygmunt Bauman (1989). These questions matter, for if we decide that human rights are just a sophisticated form of rhetoric, they do not have the political significance attributed to them, or the kind of power a human rights regime confers.

As mentioned earlier for Arendt, by contrast, the Nazis represented the breakdown of the Enlightenment and democracy, and hence of critical judgment and reason. The ambivalence between the tropes of civilization and barbarism remained the primary organizing principle of her thoughts on the Holocaust. Nazism, for her, was not particularly German but was simply one manifestation of totalitarianism. Universalizing the phenomenon did not prevent her from recognizing its singular features. She saw the uniqueness of the Holocaust not only in its scope and the systematic nature of the killings but in the attempt to deny humanity as such. Conventional categories of crime become irrelevant, a view that was later incorporated into the legal canon through the concept of crimes against humanity (Levy and Sznaider 2004).

FORGIVENESS IN TRANSITIONAL JUSTICE

The issue of forgiveness takes on different meanings when situated in the context of state practices. Despite, or perhaps because of, the pervasive trend of public apologies and forms of national introspection, we need to differentiate between the political circumstances in which these practices take place. The relative success of restitution measures depends considerably on specific regime constellations. In particular, countries (notably the post-Communist cases) under conditions of transitional justice and faced with the daunting task of becoming stable democracies frequently need to strike a balance between the search for justice and the need for civil and political stability (Mansfield and Snyder 1995; Snyder and Vinjamuri 2003). The example of postwar Germany underscores how little effect official restitution attempts had on preventing former Nazis from playing a part in rebuilding the country. It was only later, during the late 1960s, when successful reconstruction and political stability were achieved, that the pervasive failure to punish former Nazis became unacceptable. It took another two decades before the historical spotlight focused directly on the deeds of the perpetrators (as opposed to the routinized official ritual of mourning its victims).

The political expediency of this course of events is not confined to Germany or the postwar context. Discussing the recent initiative to create a Museum of Baathist Crimes in Iraq, Elizabeth Cole (2003) writes, "Numerous studies have shown that reconciliation—the rebuilding of deeply damaged relations between nations, peoples, or faiths—can begin only when peace and stability have been achieved. Once the right conditions are in place, a nation can begin to debate its past. Countries acquainted with difficult transitions can provide expertise on the traditional tools of reconciliation, from the establishment of truth commissions (South Africa, Guatemala), to the creation of documentation centers (Cambodia) on the years of violence. . . . In the early days of reconstruction, might Iraq in fact be better off focusing on its distant rather than recent past?" There is, in other words, another memory practice, that of "restorative forgetting" (Booth 2001). The widely criticized practice of de-Baathification speaks directly to the political expediency inherent in the tension between forgiveness and justice. Thus the question shifts from a quest for absolute justice to one in which states look for the best outcome possible at a given time and in light of available resources.[1] "Best" can be assessed only against the available alternatives, and not in terms of how far they fall short of ultimate goals such as human rights or justice. At issue is the fact that there is no internal contradiction between humanitarian goals and the principles of realpolitik, but there can be between human rights and realpolitik. The two may be at odds, since human rights are an absolutist framework whose principles admit no compromise. This framework provides a set of standards against which all governments can be measured, and against which all will fall short. Arguably this is appropriate and effective in its proper context, but it may be inappropriate in the context of providing peace and stability. This may be one of the fundamental reasons why successor governments must always be formed out of at least some preexisting element. The basic strategy will almost always be to back some safe candidates, make acceptable compromises with others, and arrest and exclude entirely a small minority who make compromise impossible. This last group must by definition be small or the operation cannot possibly be accomplished in a limited period of time. Thus, at times, amnesties appear to be the right political choice.

The de facto amnesty granted to Nazi officials after the war cannot possibly be squared with the demands of justice, and it loomed large during these processes. Nevertheless, amnesty remains colored by local issues. Adam Michnik and his fellow activists, who engendered the transformation in Poland, operated under the slogan "Amnesty Yes. Amnesia No" (Michnik and Havel 1993). Debates about the acceptable balance between memory and prosecution are ultimately shaped by the requirements of social and political stability. Amnesties will always contain groups and members of the former regime who are seriously compromised in human rights terms. This is also, however, where forgiveness as a political principle may come in. A human rights framework that knows no compromise or that sees any trade-off as a damnable dilution of its principles is completely unsuited to applying such a strategy. This is especially important in ethnic struggles all over the globe today.

And it is why in political terms the human rights regime has to adjust to political expediencies if it is to be effective—even if this is a paradoxical, even an absurd, demand, given that human rights came into existence to counteract political expediency. The public debate about whether the ICC should issue a warrant for the arrest of the president of Sudan, Omar Hassan Ahmad al-Bashir, for war crimes and crimes against humanity is a case in point and a cautionary tale. After protracted international talks that overlaid a human rights imperative onto the political volatility of Sudan, the ICC issued a warrant for al-Bashir's arrest in April 2009. Al-Bashir's first reaction was to ban a number of human rights organizations from Sudan.

Cautioning against the complexities of the demands imposed by human rights imperatives and the institutional requirements of transitional justice should not be construed as an argument against human rights trials as such. Much depends on local circumstances. Kim and Sikkink show that human rights trials are not necessarily detrimental to the establishment of law and order. Analyzing human rights trials in a hundred countries that experienced some form of transitional justice, they found that "transitional countries with human rights trials are less repressive than countries without trials, holding other factors constant. Contrary to the arguments made by realists, transitional human rights trials have not tended to exacerbate human rights violations. Countries with more accumulated years of trials after transition are less repressive than countries with less accumulated years of trials, ceteris paribus. In addition, countries surrounded by more neighbors with transitional trials are less repressive, which may suggest a deterrence impact of trials beyond the border" (2007, 1–2). Their findings confirm the importance of focusing on the interaction of global and local conditions.

Do states after transitions grant amnesty and forgive political criminals in the name of peace and stability? Should we allow these decisions to be overturned by an international tribunal? This is the quintessential Hobbesian situation, where civil peace is often more important than morality and where it is often the only precondition that can make real morality possible. This is fundamentally the opposite of the human rights perspective, which basically assumes that civil peace can never be endangered by its activities and that no amount of mobilization, polarization, and anathematization can ever bring about a complete breakdown of the state but always only purify it. The ultimate reality of the situation is the needs of peace, which means the realities of power. This is an argument in favor of flexible principles, whose essence is to find the best solution given the constraints of the situation and the likelihood at any point of making things worse or less durable. These principles are designed to lead to the best compromise. They are the right principles to guide choices even when trying to reach the humanitarian goal of creating a society in which people live better, safer, freer, less fearful lives. These concerns involve weighing the benefits of remembering and acting upon past human rights abuses against the costs that such memories could incur for human rights violations in the future.

THE MNEMONICS OF FORGIVENESS

By the early 1990s, the Nuremberg principles were looming large in both the international reaction to mass atrocities and in their legal inscription in the ICC (Levy and Sznaider 2004). However, the broader significance of these trials and the emerging legalism should not be reduced to its adjudicatory functions. As W. James Booth points out in his study on the relationship between justice and remembrance, trials are not only arenas of forgiveness but forums in which "justice and memory resist the passage of time and deny to it any power of moral/legal absolution." Thus "justice becomes the memory of evil, and it fights a desperate battle against the oblivion that always threatens to engulf it, that gives sanctuary to the perpetrators and a victory to injustice" (2001, 779).

In many ways, legal manifestations of forgiveness are but one facet of the issue. No less important are memories of justice. Booth suggests that "justice is, in part, a form of remembrance: Memory occupies a vital place at the heart of justice and its struggle to keep the victims, crimes, and perpetrators among the unforgotten" (777). He writes that "justice as the institutionalized remembrance of the past is seen here, as in other truth commissions, as a duty to the dead and as a condition of reconciliation"

(778). Contrary to those who view memory as merely ephemeral, Booth argues that "this memory-justice at once informs core judicial practices and ranges beyond them in a manner that leaves judicial closure incomplete. It reminds us of a duty to keep crimes and their victims from the oblivion of forgetting, of a duty to restore, preserve, and acknowledge the just order of the world" (777). This view is evidenced in the mnemonic turn that has taken place in the past twenty years, in which forgiveness has been inflated by new dimensions such as healing, reconciliation, restitution, peace, and truth (see also Booth 2006). Memory has become the key organizer that has enabled trauma and recovery to supersede justice and its administration. Political and legal theory have taken a decisive Freudian turn (Teitel 2003), and truth commissions, public debates, and restitution claims, rather than the courtroom, now serve alone as models for this process.

RESTITUTION FOR WHOM? FROM VICTIMS AND PERPETRATORS TO OBSERVERS

One clear indication of this mnemonic turn is the emergence of a discourse about restitution measures that is no longer confined to relations between states but also involves individuals. In adhering more closely to the definition of crimes against humanity, individuals and not states become legal subjects. Restitution forms the nexus of memory, forgiveness, and justice and explains why the issue of whether restitution (especially for individuals) can be rightfully entered into the moral equation of victim and perpetrator has remained intractable. A paradigmatic example of restitution is the German-Israeli *Wiedergutmachung* (Barkan 2000). While it is often cited as an exemplary case for the healing effects of restitution measures, the respective reactions to the agreements in Germany and Israel show how difficult it is to disentangle the reconciliatory effects prompted by official forgiveness from its actual connection to the perpetrators' intentions and victims' willingness to accept it. Controversial at the time, a mere seven years after the Holocaust, the agreement almost sparked civil war in Israel (Segev 2000). It was also highly unpopular among the German population, and Germany's chancellor Konrad Adenauer put his political career at stake by pushing the measure through. In Israel, opponents often referred to it as blood money. On a deeper level, the root problem seemed to be one of money and reconciliation, but principles of market society do not have to contradict moral concerns (Sznaider 2001). The German-Jewish agreements show how money can have a mediating function in the new equation of moral equivalency. At the same time, these agreements represent a specific case of forgiveness and restitution and should not necessarily be taken as a model for other historical contexts.

Overall, despite its European origins and Western dominance, this convergence of money and morality should not be seen as a new form of moral imperialism. The discourse of restitution does not rest on some absolute, universalistic ethics but is the result of cross-cultural negotiation with the Other. This cultural dialogue also involves redefining the dichotomy between the local and the global and the antagonism between universalism and particularism. The trend toward restitution in recent years does not draw on any universal legal idea but rather on a common denominator that acknowledges local, particularistic idiosyncrasies. Forgiveness and debates about restitution do not presume a universally valid legal or normative good. But mutual recognition provides the basis for reconciliation and the foundation for a shared experience. Rather than the application of a universal morality, we are witnesses to a global genesis of conditions for forgiveness that is shaped through dialogue with the local and where an ad hoc conception of justice often incorporates a globalized human rights culture into respective local and particular negotiations.

As such, the principles of restitution and forgiveness are primarily about negotiated history, in which various groups, linked across national boundaries and cleavages, seek to overcome a conflict in a quest for a common narrative. By doing so, they also change their own identity to a certain extent and create new opportunities for political action. Only forgiveness, Hannah Arendt argued, can liberate political action from the paralyzing consequences of its own entanglements and open up new horizons for action. But here, too, a word of caution is advised: a common narrative is not common in the sense that both sides tell the same story. Instead, the recognition of different narratives is what establishes the commonality. Restitution and forgiveness need not inevitably lead to a shared narrative of erstwhile victims and perpetrators, but they acknowledge that politics may accept irreconcilable plurality as a given. Nevertheless, the issue is not communicative history or discourse ethics but memories of historical conflicts in which irreconcilable viewpoints are brought closer together through the emergence of a global vantage point of human rights that involves a third party—namely, humanity as witness and bystander.

9

EAST MEETS WEST:
EUROPE AND ITS OTHERS

The most comprehensive example of countries relinquishing aspects of their sovereignty to supranational bodies is the adjudicatory authority individual states have conferred upon the European Union. The European Court of Human Rights and the European Convention on Human Rights illustrate the symbolic value and the juridical power that human rights can carry. The commission accepts complaints from a variety of nonstate actors, and national jurisdictions must abide by the decisions of the European court. As we have pointed out, postwar Europe is largely the product of the memory of fear. But it is important to reiterate that this does not only imply the kind of *denationalization* that characterizes some of the institutional transformations in the European Union. Rather, reactions to cosmopolitan pressures have prompted new articulations of national interests, as the example of the rise of a European Right, which has appropriated a multicultural rhetoric to defend the dominance of majority groups, shows. This *neonational* dynamic also finds expression in international relations: recent transatlantic tensions between the United States and some European nations cast doubt on how much diversity European universalism can tolerate; another realm in which national narratives seem to evoke earlier juxtapositions to cosmopolitanism is evidenced in the dissimultaneity of memory cultures that reflect ongoing tensions between western and eastern Europe, the subject of the first section of this chapter. Another dimension relates to a *renationalization* in which national memories of past atrocities serve cosmopolitan purposes and vice versa. Here we encounter a paradox whereby universal dispositions are deployed to reinforce particular orientations. We discuss this dynamic in the second section in a case study of how memories of expulsions in Germany have shifted between particular and universal references, appropriating human rights tropes to rehabilitate the nation via a universalistic narrative.

Countering a narrow cultural, geographical, and institutional focus, some theorists have suggested studying Europeanization in a global context with "an awareness of the importance of cultural dynamics; the centrality of contestations generated by multiple perspectives on issues central to European transformation" (Delanty and Rumford 2005, 7). As this section illustrates, common references to negative myths of European wars and distinctive memories of human rights abuses continue to produce a myriad of nation-specific reactions. Nevertheless, or perhaps precisely because of the persistence of particular memories, universalism remains a salient feature of European cosmopolitanism, even if its proponents explicitly reject the type of homogenizing claims that characterized earlier Enlightenment thinkers. Our historical analysis exemplifies how a moral universalism continues to emanate from the European model by generalizing its postnational aspirations as universal features rather than particular western European experiences.

This misperception operates on both the normative and analytic levels. For one thing, it tends to privilege universalism, as it emerged in a Western context, and project it onto the rest of the world (Chakrabarty 2000). As such, it frequently becomes exclusionary, precisely by paying scant attention to the widespread persistence of particularism. These features are reminiscent of the universalistic assumptions that guided modernization theories during the 1940s and 1950s. There was little normative and conceptual space to account for ethnic or religious particularities. They were treated as residual categories, and as evidence that backward particularism stood in the way of progress. Some current scholarly responses to retribalization and religious fundamentalism even suggest that Western secularization, along with aspirations to separate church and state, was never really the norm and is increasingly the exception. With the end of the cold war this imbalance came to the fore, as western Europe increasingly focused on memories of the Holocaust, and negative features of nationhood have been complemented by central and eastern European moves to extend memories of victimhood beyond World War II.

Many of the postwar tropes articulated by Karl Jaspers shape contemporary debates about the nature of Europeanness and the precarious balance of universal and particular modes of remembrance. Overall, European cosmopolitanism retains a strong universalistic penchant, drawing on a narrow western European experience. Jaspers's postwar vision of a core Europe propelled by France, Germany, and the Benelux countries, the rejection of nation-centric politics, the commitment to spread Enlightenment values, the cultivation of a particular social model, and above all the "lessons" of World War II, circumscribe the contours of this western European cosmopolitanism. For the most part, it is still predicated on a sense of universalism and a missionary vision that brackets particularism by seeking to homogenize what is essentially a Europe of plural and contentious voices.

But more is at stake here than different visions of universalism, because different versions of how to translate human rights rhetoric into concrete politics can contend with one another. When the United States went to war against Iraq and later tried to justify it on human rights grounds, European intellectuals distanced themselves from American interventionism. Clearly, different memories come into play here. While the American memory of World War II is the memory of liberation— with Iraq neatly playing the role of Nazi Germany in this scenario—the European memory, which itself is divided between western and eastern Europe, is a memory of devastation and destruction. While American memory claims that military action is necessary to implement a human rights regime, European memory sees a strong connection between that regime and a peaceful world of interdependence, which ironically was implemented by the Americans in western Europe as part of the new European order after the 1945 armistice.

A telling example of the different memories underpinning these competing approaches is a manifesto published in May 2003 (reprinted

in 2005) by Jürgen Habermas and Jacques Derrida that aimed to con-
solidate a European public sphere.[1] What was intended to be a reevaluation of transatlantic relations based on distinctive conceptions of how
human rights and international law should be deployed in global politics
quickly turned into a European affair in which new mnemonic divisions
between East and West came to the fore. Habermas and Derrida argued
that "contemporary Europe has been shaped by the experience of the
totalitarian regimes of the twentieth century and by the Holocaust—the
persecution and the annihilation of European Jews in which the National
Socialist regime made the societies of the conquered countries complicit
as well. Self-critical controversies about this past remind us of the moral
basis of politics. . . . A bellicose past once entangled all European nations
in bloody conflicts. They drew a conclusion from that military and spiritual mobilization against one another: the imperative of developing new,
supranational forms of cooperation after the Second World War. The successful history of the European Union may have confirmed Europeans
in their belief that the domestication of state power demands a mutual
limitation of sovereignty, on the global as well as the national-state level"
(2005, 11–12).

The manifesto also invoked the notion of a core Europe, relegating
both the British and the countries in the process of joining the EU to
a secondary role. Membership, so the argument implied, should rely
primarily on secular European Enlightenment values and social democratic traditions. The underlying idea was to generalize the experiences
of France, Germany, and the Benelux countries and posit them as the
standard-bearer for European integration. For Habermas and Derrida,
the "EU already offers itself as a form of 'governance beyond the nation-
state,' which could set a precedent in the post-national constellation.
And for decades, European social welfare systems served as a model.
Certainly, they have now been thrown on the defensive at the level of
the nation-state. Yet future political efforts at the domestication of global
capitalism must not fall below the standards of social justice that they
established. If Europe has solved two problems of this magnitude, why
shouldn't it issue a further challenge: to defend and promote a cosmopolitan order on the basis of international law, against competing visions?"

(7–8). Parodying this European cosmopolitanism, the Hungarian writer Peter Esterhazy replied to the manifesto, "Once, I was an Eastern European; then I was promoted to the rank of Central European. Then a few months ago, I became a New European. But before I had the chance to get used to this status—even before I could have even refused it—I have now become a non-Core European. It's like someone who has always lived in Munkács, and has never left Munkács in his entire life and who is, nevertheless, a one-time Hungarian, one-time Czech, one-time citizen of the Soviet Union, then a citizen of the Ukraine. In our town, this is how we become cosmopolitans" (2005, 74).

A closer look shows that much of the postnational universalism that informs this western European vision clashes with a polyvocal Europe and cannot be resolved by recourse to slogans about unity in diversity. This is not a substantial argument about the virtues of a specific social model, the historical centrality of World War II, the critical assessment of public religiosity,[2] or a particular understanding of globalization. Instead, this core European version of cosmopolitanism seeks to flatten the continuous divisions in Europe including the mnemonic divide between East and West, rather than acknowledge particular Otherness as key features of European diversity. In many ways, as the immediate reactions to the manifesto have shown, talk about European integration has become a barometer for disagreement in Europe, and one that is especially pertinent in the context of European expansion. Here the divergent historical memories of existing and prospective EU member states are largely ignored. Faced with this nonrecognition, many of the new member states from the East seek to garner legitimacy for their particular experiences and memories. Most notably, they disavow the centrality of the Holocaust in favor of their own victimhood under Stalinism (Krzeminski 2005).

This clash of memories is especially acute when we consider how the West perceives the East, how the East looks at how the West views the East, and how the East itself is reconfiguring its historical memories in the context of European integration. Most Western conceptualizations of Europe tend to neglect the contributions of central, eastern, and non-European pasts (Delanty 2003). Western perceptions of the East

sometimes resonate with an older Orientalizing discourse in which the
East simply represents the uncivilized Other. For instance, the German
historian Hans-Ulrich Wehler pointed out, "White Russia, the Ukraine
. . . , Moldova, Russia itself, and Turkey in particular have never been
part of a historic Europe. They do not live off the legacy of Judaic, Greek
or Roman antiquity that is present in Europe to this day. They have not
fought their way through the far-reaching separation of state and church,
or even return, as they did after the Bolshevist or Kemalist intermezzo,
to a symbiotic relationship between the two. They have not experienced
any Reformation and, even more importantly, hardly any Enlightenment.
They have produced no European bourgeoisie, no autonomous European
bourgeois cities, no European nobility, and no European peasantry. They
have not participated in the greatest achievement of European political
culture since the late nineteenth century: the construction of the social
welfare state" (2005, 121).

Less blatant, but in line with a generalized perception of Europe and
its civilizing mission, are the postnational visions that characterize the
expectations of core European states. "And the central and eastern European countries, while certainly working hard for their admission into
the EU, are nevertheless not yet ready to place limits on the sovereignty
that they have so recently regained" (Habermas and Derrida 2005, 5).
Whereas Hans Kohn's (1944/2005) classic dichotomy of civic Western
and primordial Eastern nationalism set the tone for the first half of the
twentieth century, a new binary discourse has emerged that celebrates
Western postnationalism and condemns the persistence or return of ethnic, religious, and/or national particularism in the East or anywhere else,
for that matter. It seems ironic these days that Kohn's dichotomy between
"good" postnational, civic nationhood and "bad" ethnic nationalism took
the United States, where the contradiction between rights and sovereignty was dissolved, as its chief model. More than half a century later,
contemporary political realities are realigning historical memories. Eastern European ethnic nation-states now share an affinity with the United
States in ways that postnational western Europe does not. This brings
us back to the cold war and the liberalism of fear. The cold war made it
imperative for the United States to support the human rights activities

of eastern European dissidents, while western European states and intellectuals were content with a politics of appeasement with the states of the Warsaw Pact. Memories of war, destruction, and desolation prevailed over memories of totalitarianism, which is also the major divide between eastern and western Europe.[3] This has consequences for the politics of human rights as well.

The civilizational undertones and Western superiority that is common to most of these statements resonates with the heated discussions about and restrictive policies related to European enlargement. Eastern European intellectuals and politicians, responding to the idea of a core Europe, resent both the assumed superiority of the West and the way it perceives let alone has treated the East. The need to fulfill a long list of political and economic conditions before being allowed to join the EU, as well as negotiations over full freedom for labor to move across Europe and the recent constitutional failures, have all contributed to a sense of being second-class citizens in the European project. Adam Krzeminski, an important public intellectual and publisher in Poland, in an essay entitled "First Kant, Now Habermas," notes that, "whereas the USA was organized democratically from the very beginning, Europe seems to maintain its feudal framework. Over centuries, it had been built according to the principle of seniority. And even now, it is frightened that the barbarians have captured the outer walls of the EU. After all, the economic and spiritual warriors of the Occident are attempting to retreat into the redoubt of 'Core Europe,' probably in the hope that hosts of angels will provide for relief. Politically, they wish to remain among themselves as 'avant-garde'; economically, they think of tightening the Maastricht criteria for the Euro-zone so that none of the poor can intrude. And finally, the latter are also deliberately excluded from a philosophical dispute concerning Europe's spirit" (2005, 147).

This sense of exclusion is also evident in eastern Europe's looking-glass self, in how, that is, the East thinks it is perceived by the West. Andrzej Stasiuk, a Polish writer, describing "the map of the territory of two hundred million future Europeans," writes sarcastically, "The plan for the coming decades looks more or less like this: the Sinti will arrive with their wagons and will set up camp in the middle of the Champs-Elysées;

Bulgarian bears will perform their tricks on Berlin's Kudamm; half-wild Ukrainians will encamp their misogynistic Cossack troops on the plain of the Po before the gates of Milan; drunken Poles rapt in prayer will ravage the vineyards of the Rhine and Mosel and will plant bushes that bear fruit full of pure denatured alcohol and then move on; they will sing their litanies and will not stop until they reach the edge of the continent in the arch-Catholic Santiago de Compostela, famous for its miracles. It is difficult to say what the Romanians will do with their millions of sheep. They are a people known especially for their sheep breeding, but also for their unpredictability. Serbs, Croatians and Bosnians will cross the English Channel in Dalmatian dug-out canoes and balkanize Britain, which will finally be divided as God commanded it, into Scotland, England and Wales" (2005, 103–4). This caricature is not merely a sardonic comment but also a stark reminder of how the salience of Otherness, along with ethnic, religious, and national inflections, is complicating cosmopolitan imageries.

Nowhere is this more apparent than in the mnemonic divide that is emblematic of East-West relations and the fact that the cosmopolitanization of Europe is a work in progress rather than a progressive vision based on a set of universalistic principles. In his writings on postwar European memory, Tony Judt points out that the Holocaust and the murder of European Jewry play a marginal role in post-Communist eastern Europe, mirroring the bracketing of Jewish victimhood in the postwar period. Much of this is the product of how Communist regimes in the postwar era, not unlike their western counterparts, excluded references to Jews, preferring to remember World War II as an epic struggle against fascism. "There were national categories ('Hungarians') and above all social categories ('workers'), but ethnic and religious tags were studiously avoided. The Second World War was labeled and taught as an anti-fascist war; its racist dimension was ignored. . . . But if East Europeans paid less attention in retrospect to the plight of the Jews it was not just because they were indifferent at the time or preoccupied with their own survival. It is because the Communists imposed enough suffering and injustice of their own to forge a whole new layer of resentments and memories" (2005, 823).

To be sure, the East-West dichotomy itself is not contained within fixed geographical boundaries. It is also increasingly part of domestic debates in eastern and central Europe itself. State-imposed commemorative practices became the subject of fiery debates in the aftermath of Communism, contributing to the renationalization of memories and a challenge to the Holocaust-centered narrative of the West. It was a development compounded by post-Communist memories of Stalinism and corresponding forms of *Vergangenheitsbewältigung* (coming to terms with the past). As Judt points out, overcoming Communism was accomplished by inverting it. "What had once been official truth was now discredited root and branch—becoming, as it were, officially false. But this sort of taboo-breaking carries its own risks. Before 1989 every anti-Communist had been tarred with the 'Fascist' brush. But if 'anti-Fascism' had been just another Communist lie, it was very tempting now to look with retrospective sympathy and even favor upon *all* hitherto discredited anti-Communists, Fascists included. Nationalist writers of the 1930s returned to fashion" (824). In short, it is the rediscovery of long delegitimized forms of nationalism transported through memory politics that themselves are part of a Europeanizing process.

This renationalization has been matched by a growing resentment toward the West for privileging memories of the Holocaust and paying little attention to the suffering in the Stalinist Gulag. "With this post-Communist reordering of memory in Eastern Europe, the taboo on comparing communism with Nazism began to crumble. Indeed, politicians and scholars started to insist upon such comparisons. In the West this juxtaposition remained controversial. . . . To many Western European intellectuals Communism was a failed variant of a common progressive heritage. But to their Central and East European counterparts it was an all too successful local application of the criminal pathologies of authoritarianism and should be remembered thus. Europe might be united, but European memory remained deeply asymmetrical" (ibid., 826). This transformation and pluralization of memory regimes makes a singular and unifying notion of European cosmopolitanism highly controversial.

Underlying these contested memories is a continuous balancing of competing conceptions of victimhood. National memories tend to privilege their own victims. Owing to these transformations, however, cosmopolitanized memories complicate matters insofar as they contribute to an emerging duality, because nations have to engage with both their status as victims and their role as perpetrators. Competing conceptions of victimhood are thrust into a dynamic that oscillates between denationalization and renationalization, comparable to the tension between universal human rights and specific privileges. On the one hand, the European gaze rejects clear-cut perpetrator-victim distinctions and any hierarchy of victimhood, stressing the virtues of dialogue among the different parties. On the other hand, it is precisely this absence of a hierarchy of victims that decontextualizes and at times dehistoricizes the actual deeds of past injustices. We are not supposed to distinguish between the respective sufferings of groups, and every attempt to privilege one group over another is met with strong resistance. Leveling the field of suffering also has unintended consequences, as it challenges existing beliefs about who the perpetrators and who the victims are.

The central problem with this vision is not merely that it limits cosmopolitanism to a particular western European experience but that it tends to denigrate the particularism of others as an affront to its postnational vision of politics. Despite its declared commitment to recognizing Otherness, core-European cosmopolitanism has fallen back into established patterns of Othering. Operating within old antinomies of cosmopolitanism versus nationalism, the eastern European resurgence of national narratives is one relationship onto which core Europeans project this new universalism. As such, an imagined East "has been cut loose from its geographical point of reference and has become a generalised social marker in European identity formation" (Neumann 1999, 207). This is not the sole manifestation of alterity that serves as a tool for the consolidation of a core-European cosmopolitanism.

European values—the social democratic model, postnational human rights, and limited state sovereignty—have been contrasted with American society (i.e., American religiosity, limited welfare, and unabashed patriotism) and politics (e.g., bellicose American policies, privileging national interest over international law). The disjuncture between valuable suggestions about theorizing Europe in the context of global processes

(Delanty and Rumford 2005; Beck and Grande 2007) and the rejection of globalization through an identification with Americanization (Beck, Sznaider, and Winter 2004) could not be starker. Core Europeans continue to Orientalize the Other and "are still caught in the trap of a binary moral geography. To varying degrees, their polarizing ideological narrative seeks to freeze authoritatively the meaning of 'Europe' by expurgating its Other, which is now 'America'" (Heins 2006, 1).

The transatlantic rift and the East-West divide are complemented by the widespread rejection of Europe's domestic Others, namely, its Muslim population. Inverting previous multicultural ideas and policies that celebrate particularism, many European states and intellectuals now reject Islamic traditions by portraying them in their most particularistic extremes. Universalist fundamentalism continues to be at the root of much cosmopolitan thinking, and this is not only analytically misleading but politically unpersuasive. While the cosmopolitanization of Europe continues to dissolve physical borders, European cosmopolitanism is, if not intentionally then in effect, redrawing moral boundaries. Europe emerges against the backdrop of a cosmopolitan order that commands political attention to human rights. However, cosmopolitanization unfolds unevenly against competing memories, which are circumscribing perceptions of rights and their political significance.

THE EUROPEANIZATION OF NATIONHOOD: UNIVERSAL SUFFERING

Shifting official memories of ethnic cleansing in Germany provide a good example of the ways in which memories of human rights abuses are subject to reinterpretation. German memories of expulsions have veered from particular and universal references to recent attempts to rehabilitate the nation via a universal narrative. The German case also speaks to a more general trend in the relationship between minority and human rights. As we saw in chapter 5, postwar developments marked a departure from minority rights and a move toward human rights. Contemporary manifestations of this relationship are different insofar as human rights and memories of past atrocities are fused with and inscribed in minority politics. The old tension and even contradiction between group rights and individual rights is being transcended in current human rights discourse. In his comparative study on reparation politics, Elazar Barkan (2000) refers to this as "Neo-Enlightenment"—a trend whereby individual rights are transferred to groups or minorities, which are treated as individuals writ large. The outcome is to bring Paine and Burke together under one theoretical umbrella. One of the consequences is that in current political discourse human and minority rights are used interchangeably and without distinction.

Images of German victims have become a ubiquitous feature of political debates and mass-mediated cultural events in recent years. The changing representations of the Holocaust and the emergence of a human rights discourse have served as a political and cultural prism through which histories of German victimhood have been renegotiated. More specifically, the centrality of the Holocaust in Germany informs how the postwar expulsion of twelve million ethnic Germans has been remembered. Most interpretations of the destruction of European Jewry and the expulsion of ethnic Germans from Poland and Czechoslovakia, and their corresponding memory cultures, treat these memories as mutually exclusive manifestations of competing perceptions of national self-image. Yet memories of both the Holocaust and expulsions are entwined. The Holocaust remains a specific event but also spans a universalizing human rights discourse that conceals the magnitude of the Holocaust as a particular historical occurrence; at the same time, the expulsion ceases being a particular event and is reframed as a universal evil known as ethnic cleansing. The way in which expulsions of ethnic Germans have been politicized and remembered in recent debates reveals how comparisons with other occurrences of state-sanctioned violence and claims of singularity shape the balance of universal and particular modes of commemoration.

Moreover, these debates shed light on how memories of past injustices forge an emerging global human rights discourse that revolves around the denationalization of historical memories and attempts to renationalize Germany's political culture. Representations of the Holocaust are no longer confined to particular national histories. Elsewhere we have elaborated on how the assumed link between collective memory and nationhood is modified in the context of globalization, and leads to the emergence of cosmopolitanized memories (Levy and Sznaider 2005). Not only are memory cultures no longer constrained by national boundaries; they are also negotiated with reference to narratives generated outside the nation. Collective memories of the Holocaust in Europe serve as an admonition that when modernity develops exclusively within the nation-state, it bears the potential for moral, political, economic, and technological catastrophe. Recent scholarship on what is now called ethnic cleansing frequently espouses the same view. It is the connection to the modern nation-state and its radical exclusivist forms that pushes the Holocaust to the forefront in discussions of ethnic cleansing and, consequently, informs debates on expulsions (Mazower 1999; Naimark 2002; Preece 1998).

How has the tension between universal and particular readings of past injustices informed the ways in which representations of German victimhood and expulsions in particular have been transformed? The Holocaust can simultaneously be constitutive for a European outlook as well as for a more nationalistic perspective. The Europeanization of the Holocaust in Germany reveals a double bind. On the one hand, it attempts to universalize while retaining the *Sonderweg* (German special path) perspective that implies Germany's unique trajectory toward and responsibility for the Holocaust. On the other hand, the same process of Europeanization also serves as a mechanism to depart from this *Sonderweg* and, paradoxically, leads to a renationalization of Germany through the discourse of Europeanization.

A key component of the organization of collective memory is the perceived victim status of a group. The universal idea of victimhood begins with the idea that modern warfare makes everyone victims. It does not matter if you start, win, or lose the war, because war is a human tragedy affecting all. This is why, in the universalized discourse of victimhood, war is seen as a tragedy and a deviation from the cosmopolitan path to peace. In universalized victimhood, there is no ultimate difference between victors and vanquished—World War II made victims of them all—whereas in Jewish Holocaust victim consciousness, there is an essential divide between victims and perpetrators. In short, war makes everyone a victim, while genocide and ethnic cleansing imply a focus on a perpetrator and a victim. This yields two parallel and somewhat incompatible conceptions of victim consciousness, one universal and one particular. The particular highlights the crimes of the aggressor and the universal downplays the crimes through the very idea that we are all victims. The particular form of victim consciousness depends on the distinction between perpetrator and victim. Thus, under the particular system, there can be no victim without a perpetrator, and, conversely, to call someone a victim is instantly to accuse someone else of being a perpetrator. In this view, there are deserving and undeserving victims.

Particularism concentrates on the aggressors and justifies war and revenge as the means by which victims cease to be victims and become aggressors, thereby achieving justice. In the universalist conception, where the ultimate goal is the creation of a world without war, the concentration on perpetrators undercuts the whole idea of victim consciousness; all victims are deserving. This stance is evident not only in the debates about the suffering of the German expellees but also in the recent renewed attention to the memory of German suffering resulting from the Allied bombing campaign. Here, too, questions of universality versus particularity arise. Are these victims members of a specific group belonging to a former collective of perpetrators, or are they individuals, as in victims of crimes against humanity? Given that representations of expulsion are located in the contentious field of cosmopolitanizing and renationalizing forms of remembrance, what is the role of global human rights ideals for national modes of legitimacy? How is the national reconfigured against the backdrop of Europeanized memories? Questions about ways to balance the subject of expulsion and the particular fate of German expellees, on the one hand, and those expelled and exterminated by Germans, on the other, have become a central theme in public and political discourse, which also informs the East-West divide.

The Potsdam Treaty of 1945 sanctioned large population transfers after the war that resulted in the flight and expulsion of about twelve million ethnic Germans from eastern and central Europe who are now commonly referred to as expellees (*Vertriebene*). It should be noted that the term, introduced along with the federal expellee law in 1953, is a charged concept connoting a certain status of victimhood. Before that, ethnic Germans were referred to as refugees, a reference that situated their history in a broader migratory context. While the term "expellees" is well entrenched in German discourse, some scholars have recently suggested narrating the history of ethnic German expulsion within a more universal context of forced migration that would address issues in a European or even a global history of migrations (Ahonen 2003). The map of Europe and not only Europe was redrawn after World War II. Population transfer was considered the solution to the problem of nationalities and irredentism resulting from the breakdown of the minority protection system of the League of Nations. After World War II Europe experienced a refugee crisis on a grand scale (see Judt 2005, 22ff.). Entire population groups were deported to the East by the Soviet Union. Italians living on the Istrian peninsula left or were made to return to Italy, and Italian life in Yugoslavia thus came to an end. People fled retribution or ethnic homogenization. Bulgaria transferred Turks to Turkey, Czechoslovakia exchanged ethnic populations with Hungary, Poland and Lithuania "switched" populations, but it was the German expellees who caught the imagination of postwar discourse.

This is the political and cultural background for most of the debates since the end of the bipolar world, which have been characterized by two key features since the late 1990s. Earlier tropes of competing victimhood have been revived, albeit under different geopolitical and normative circumstances. Memories of expulsion and self-conscious debates about how to commemorate them are now taking place within the context of an expanding European Union. Different mnemonic entrepreneurs are trying to Europeanize the theme of expulsion. Of particular interest is the fact that these attempts are simultaneously driven by those who seek to denationalize collective memories and by groups, usually on the right of the political spectrum in Germany, that employ narratives of European victimhood as a way to renationalize memories. These are the moral entrepreneurs who attempted to create a Center Against Expulsion (*Zentrum gegen Vertreibung*)—a memorial purposely not unlike Holocaust memorials to the Germans who were forced to leave their homes in eastern Europe and relocate in the German motherland. The controversies surrounding the design and location of the museum capture the exclusionary universalism of memories and how comparisons of expulsion and the Holocaust are invoked in order to renationalize collective memory. They are a very good example of the tendency to decontextualize historically specific events and recontextualize them against a general backdrop of human rights principles that are shaped by memories of desolation and of total war and its consequences.

Initially, support was sought to create such a center in the new German capital of Berlin. The plan prompted an outcry from those who suspected that this would renationalize Germany's memory culture, once again privileging German suffering at the expense of that of Others. Some suggested Europeanizing the center by locating it in a Polish city that was part of Germany before the war. The ensuing debates revolved around the question of the proper place for such a museum and the extent to which references to expulsion should remain within the confines of national memories or whether the complicated relationship of victims and perpetrators should or could be Europeanized, revealing how collective memories of national suffering can be circumscribed by new legitimating frames attached to a transnational European idea. This dynamic in turn was supported by the emergence of a human rights frame, which served many of the protagonists in these debates as a constitutive moment of a cosmopolitanized memoryscape. But this universal frame of reference does not necessarily imply a denationalization of memory politics; in fact, it frequently facilitates renationalization.

Cosmopolitanization can also entail a distinctive future-oriented dimension in which it is not a memory that looks only to the past to produce a new formative myth. Discussions about postnational collectivities focus mostly on the future. Cosmopolitanized memories are based largely on the desire to prevent or limit future suffering. The theme of expulsion becomes a constitutive moment for a common European past that is envisioned as a possible foundation for a shared European system of values predicated on a human rights discourse and a de-territorialized memory of the fate of all victims. Memory here becomes synonymous with the idea of a shared culture and becomes the main reason for reminding people of the expulsions.

In October 2000 the Goethe Institute, Germany's international cultural institution, invited Günter Grass, Czeslaw Milosz, Wislawa Szymborska, and Tomas Vonclova to meet in Vilna, where they discussed the trauma of expulsion and the dangers of nationalism. That meeting resulted in a publication entitled *Die Zukunft der Erinnerung* (The Future of Memory) that essentially prefigured many of the positions that would come to characterize the objections to the proposed center in Berlin. For instance, Milosz took the opportunity to reminisce about the cosmopolitan character of the prewar Vilna of his youth, praising its multiethnic composition and warning against attempts to privilege national memories. Milosz argued that contemporary central European memories must acknowledge this multiplicity and recognize the presence of the Other. Here the past of the ethnic nation and the postwar experience of homogenization were suppressed in favor of a cosmopolitan past and the necessity to deploy the past for future benefits. But this position was just that: one literary voice in a broader European discourse that was not confined to attempts at denationalization but actually resorted to Europe in order to advance a national perspective. The dispute that erupted between Germany and Poland about the location of the proposed center is emblematic of the precarious balance between victimhood and perpetrators. It also highlights the paradoxical effect of Europeanization.

Germany's official political culture since the early 1970s has created a public discourse in which narratives about German suffering are not easily voiced without a direct causal reference to German crimes before the expulsions. Without such a reference, one is labeled nationalistic. Here lies one crucial difference with the postwar commemoration of expulsion. During the first two postwar decades, Germany's official discourse emphasized the suffering of Germans without much reference to the aggression that preceded and ultimately caused retributions against Germans. Hence, the question of commemorating German victims remains a charged issue, for it has always harbored the potential to come at the expense of a full recognition of the deeds perpetrated by Germans during

World War II. Accordingly, every time German victimhood is thematized, it is accompanied by the insistence that it is not intended to relativize Germany's role as perpetrator. Not unlike the discursive parallels between postwar reactions and attempts during the 1980s to revive certain conceptions of victimhood, in the past few years renewed attention has shifted to a comparison of perpetrators. A good example is a study by Wilhelm Heitmeyer (2004), which reported that in a recent survey of Germans, 51 percent of respondents said that there is not much difference between what Israel is doing to the Palestinians today and what the Nazis did to the Jews during the Holocaust. Furthermore, 68 percent believe that Israel is waging a "war of extermination" against the Palestinians.

The tension between historically specific events and the general phenomenon of expulsion continuously circumscribes the debates about the proposed center. Is it about the recognition of German victims, who should simultaneously be grouped with the perpetrators? Or is it about directing responsibility toward eastern European countries? Is the expulsion of German victims a direct consequence of their own role as perpetrators, or are we to remember expulsions as isolated acts of injustice? It is here that we observe repeated invocations of a human rights frame. That there is a near consensus on the European idea was articulated by Michael Jeismann, writing in the *Frankfurter Allgemeine Zeitung*:

> Remembering together and not against each other is the appeal of the shared "Danzig Declaration" by President Johannes Rau and the Polish president Aleksander Kwasniewski in October 2003. Nations are supposed to remember in such a way that the political Europe is not weakened but strengthened. All the demands together are so different, and in part so contradictory, that it is difficult to imagine how they could all be satisfied. In the long run, though, at least based on the experience with national memory cultures, those memories that are politically the most usable become dominant. The framework for a politically useful memory, it can be assumed, will be a European reference to human rights, to which the memory of the murder of European Jews is already attuned. (2004, 41)

Expulsions are increasingly decontextualized and subsumed under a broader human rights category that owes its recent prominence to the iconographic status of Holocaust memories. This point is also echoed in the open letter of May 14, 2002, in the Polish daily *Gazeta Wyborcza* that Adam Krzeminski and Adam Michnik addressed to the German chancellor and Polish prime minister. Defending Wroclaw as the ideal location for a center commemorating the German expellees, they wrote, "it would be neither a museum exclusively focusing on German suffering and German accusations, that would transform perpetrators into victims, nor would it be a museum of Polish martyrdom and colonization, but a museum of catastrophe and a sign for the renewal of our common Europe. . . . With all the suffering that we have inflicted upon each other—if in an asymmetrical fashion—it is precisely this tragedy which has again bound us together." Typical of many of the positions regarding the center is the recognition of expulsion as a crime against human rights, which points to the centrality of transnational modes of legitimation. The human rights frame also typifies a third position that proposes a more fragmented approach to the center rather than a decision for a particular location.

To underscore the universal character of these violations, references are made to the "century of expulsions" and genocidal events predating the Holocaust, such as the Armenian case. Expulsions are increasingly perceived as a global theme that must be addressed and remembered outside the parameters of national commemoration. Most of the newspaper articles and parliamentary sessions we analyzed saw the debate about the center as a trigger for a denationalized orientation toward human rights. Although, or possibly because, the controversy originally revolved around the bilateral relations between Germany and Poland, a majority who favored the cosmopolitanization of the project argued for a nation-transcending narrative as a foundational moment for a European memoryscape.

However, it should be reiterated that the adherence to a European framework and other nation-transcending modes of legitimation can also operate as a way to renationalize memory. The German controversy about expulsions is closely tied to the way the Holocaust is remembered.

Those who wish to understand the Holocaust in comparative perspective often regard the widespread claim of its singularity as constraining the return to self-confident nationhood. The revisionist Right seeks to reverse this by situating the German experience in a comparative framework that revives the cold war vocabulary of totalitarianism, aiming to shift attention from the Holocaust as a unique event to one amenable to comparisons.

A universal human rights framework that puts memories of the Holocaust on the same level as the remembrance of German expellees has multiple meanings that are determined within the parameters of cosmopolitanization and renationalization. Renewed efforts to integrate the extermination of European Jewry and the expulsion of ethnic Germans are now part of a pervasive human rights discourse. This is a double-edged sword, and it allows representations of the Holocaust that carry dual meanings. The new interpretation of ethnic cleansing, including the view of Germans as victims trying to memorialize their victimhood, is a cosmopolitan history of multiplicities insofar as it encompasses the suffering of others in universal terms. This becomes especially true when the Holocaust is recounted as one part of a broader narrative about ethnic cleansing. Much of this relates to a broader debate about modernity and the idea of the ethnically homogenous nation-state. In this view, the Holocaust loses its German specificity and is reset in the context of modernity (Bauman 1989). Germany ceases to be the exception to the rule of European national development. What distinguished the Third Reich was not its uniqueness but its extremity. It is the ethnic nation-state that is now perceived as the quintessential evil in history. The Holocaust is subsumed under the broader category of the "century of expulsions" and, as such, is merely another, albeit more extreme, example of ethnic cleansing or genocide.

HUMAN RIGHTS AND SOVEREIGNTY AFTER 9/11

HOBBES'S RETURN: HUMAN RIGHTS, TERRORISM, AND FEAR OF/FOR THE STATE

How does an institutionalized human rights regime circumscribe sovereign politics and international relations in the context of global terrorism? As much as the end of the cold war constituted an important juncture for the consolidation of the human rights regime, the terrorist attacks of September 11, 2001, and their geopolitical aftermath have added a new urgency to debates about the political status of human rights and sovereign prerogatives (Cushman 2005). Terrorism challenges the political salience of human rights principles and frequently causes the state to revert to one of its founding imperatives: the provision of security for its citizens (Sznaider 2006). Only when people feel insecure enough do they appreciate the security the state can provide. Only when they fear nothing more than violent death will they accept the state as the ultimate protector.

Antiterrorist measures and expanding executive powers frequently infringe upon civic rights and have led some to demand that sovereignty be less conditional (Ignatieff 2004). Terrorism shifts attention away from state abuse and redirects national memories to failures of the state to protect its citizens. Despite these challenges, however, or perhaps precisely because of them, even the national interest through which antiterrorist measures are justified continues to be articulated in the global context of a human rights discourse. The recurrence of strong executive powers and national interest politics weakens international legitimacy and requires extensive justifications vis-à-vis human rights standards. Global interdependencies and the concomitant human rights rhetoric they have propelled are challenging the basic tenets of sovereignty (Beck and Grande 2007; Sassen 2006).

Thus there has been a shift in the role of fear. Whereas the liberalism of fear could spark a human rights regime based on memories of dark and totalitarian times, a new illiberalism of fear evokes memories of the state of nature and fear of violent death. Although Hobbes developed his political theory in the midst of political turmoil, current suspensions of human rights are not taking place in the middle of political crises but in the context of ongoing political reconfigurations. International terrorism is occurring at a historical moment when the classic nation-state, a state that monopolized the means of violence and whose task it was to neutralize the fear of violent death, or at least direct it into civilized channels, is being transformed. As soon as the state is recognized as the only source of legitimate violence, people internalize the state's authority as the "mortal god," to employ Hobbes's metaphor of the Leviathan. This means that the state is worshipped as the new legitimate god, replacing the sovereignty of the religious God.

Sovereign regimes, especially those that feel threatened by terrorists, tend to fall back on classic notions of statehood—that is, to adopt the principle of security from violent death. While the human rights regime is a performative principle of political virtuosity where life, liberty, and the dignity of men are the main principles, the security principle must react to fears of its citizens in order to establish its authority. To paraphrase Arendt, human rights also mean that man's rather than God's command or the commands of the state should be the source of law. Thus the human rights regime replaces another regime, which was founded on the assumption that people must relinquish their liberty in order to be safe. In a world where citizenship and solidarity are based on global interdependencies, human rights are supposed to provide the glue that binds people to one another.

Since the terrorist attacks of September 11, international politics has left the realm of calculability, and the generally accepted rules of warfare have been renegotiated. The Westphalian order, grounded on the notion that a stable and peaceful political order can be maintained only by mutually supportive vows of nonintervention between political entities, no longer holds. The modern human rights regime is premised on the notion that the prevention of human suffering takes precedence over the principle of sovereignty. This is the opposite of Hobbes's argument and runs counter to the state's claim to provide security. The perceived suffering of strangers and the impulse to alleviate that suffering is one of the unintended consequences of the global process. Yet there is built-in tension between human rights and security. Article 3 of the Universal Declaration of Human Rights clearly states, "Everyone has the right to life, liberty and security of person." Security of person has become a human right in itself. This principle may stand in complete contradiction to the first principles of the declaration: "All human beings are born free and equal in dignity and rights. They are endowed with reason and conscience and should act towards one another in a spirit of brotherhood [Article 1] and Everyone is entitled to all the rights and freedoms set forth in this Declaration, without distinction of any kind, such as race, color, sex, language, religion, political or other opinion, national or social origin, property, birth or other status. Furthermore, no distinction shall be made on the basis of the political, jurisdictional or international status of the country or territory to which a person belongs, whether it be independent, trust, non-self-governing or under any other limitation of sovereignty [Article 2]." Fear of violent death clashes automatically with the fear of the suspension of human rights. Liberty is the foundation of human rights, but liberty must be defended if human rights are to be secured.

This takes us back to the old Arendtian problem of human rights. When Arendt formulated her "perplexities of human rights" after the events of the Holocaust became known, she felt that the principles of human rights had failed to avoid the slaughter of the innocent during World War II: "The Rights of Man, after all, had been defined as 'inalienable' because they were supposed to be independent of all governments; but it turned out that the moment human beings lacked their own

government and had to fall back upon their minimum rights, no authority was left to protect them and no institution was willing to guarantee
them" (1958, 291–92). Things have changed in the age of globalization,
but the problems remain similar. Today the threat of terror is more universal than ever before. This is what connects recent terrorist acts with
the totalitarian ideologies of the twentieth century and makes Arendt's
analysis of them so starkly applicable to our dark times. Sociologists
who are used to speaking up for the injured and humiliated, regardless
of who they are, will have a hard time integrating nihilistic terrorism
within their own professional framework of reason and enlightened self-
interest. Sociology as a profession is itself a product of the social contract.

States are the foundation of international law, even though the concept of crimes against humanity undermines the state-centered outlook
of international law and stresses the notion of human rights beyond
states. At the same time, terrorism is first of all a crime against humanity, since humanity's basic principle is protection against violent death.
The initial definition of crimes against humanity specified that they were
crimes against civilian populations. It implied a personal responsibility
for crimes that goes beyond one's state loyalties. Consequently, "wars
on terrorism" cannot be the struggle of one state alone; they need to be
conducted in concert with all concerned about the survival of the social
contract. In order for that contract to survive, the modern state cannot
breach the law to save itself. This is the major challenge that states fight-
ing terrorism face today. Security and human rights are not mutually
exclusive. They cannot be, for security is a human right. As such, there
can be no league of enlightened republics working hand in hand when
people do not feel secure in their homes or outside them. This is accepting political reality without giving in to illusions.

THE SOVEREIGNTY OF HUMAN RIGHTS

This book contributes to sociological engagement with human rights as
a cosmopolitan project. Both cosmopolitanism and human rights have
been excluded from the sociological mainstream. But globalization is

creating new conditions that may lead to the global diffusion, and by extension the local incorporation, of human rights norms. We have addressed the theoretical dimension and empirical conditions of cosmopolitanization by elucidating the mechanisms through which human rights have gained prominence. Just as political contingencies circumscribe the ways in which human rights matter, so do different and related ways of engaging with memories of past abuses. A crucial facet that informs the reception or rejection of human rights and concomitant compassion or indifference relates to the dissimultaneity of memories. Memory practices are mediated by idiosyncratic group features of temporal experiences and distinctive cultural dispositions toward specific pasts and pastness in general. As Maurice Halbwachs, the founding father of memory studies, put it, "Every group—be it religious, political or economic, family, friends, or acquaintances, even a transient gathering in a salon, auditorium, or street, immobilizes time in its own way and imposes on its members the illusion that, in a given duration of a constantly changing world, certain zones have acquired a relative stability and balance in which nothing essential is altered" (1980, 126). We need to be attentive to the kind of cultural validations specific groups attribute to temporal phenomena, such as progress, change, innovation, and memory itself. And, of course, we must acknowledge the fact that groups have different experiences.

As we have argued in this book, the potential for public compassion and the salience of human rights politics are highly contingent matters. They are vastly complicated by the fact that dominant state memories have given way to a more fragmented and pluralized mnemonic landscape that is further contributing to the decoupling of nation and state. As we showed in the previous chapter, however, memory practices are mediated by distinctive experiences, and a clash of memories frequently provides the foundation around which cosmopolitan memories are organized. In the age of globalization, social and cultural differences become more apparent and can influence the ways in which memories are formed. We in no way mean to imply that the revival of ethnic identities is merely a knee-jerk reaction to the supposedly homogenizing efforts of globalization. Rather, what we are dealing with is a self-aware, reflexive outlook that recognizes the world as an arena of experiences. It involves an awareness of the welfare of others and of global conditions rather than actual contact with others. In this case, the world encroaches on the local scene, whether through events taking place at the other end of the world that influence our existence or through a vision of an interconnected world (Kurasawa 2004). These different approaches to globalization lead to a multiplicity of temporal models and, above all, to the breakdown of a time line determined by past, present, and future.

Two camps have responded to this temporal realignment: those who view the acceleration of time as a threat, and those who integrate it into their everyday experience. For those who take the latter reflexive attitude, the choice of identities is no longer necessarily based on existing continuities but rather on informed preferences. This outlook has nothing to do with evolutionary theories of modernization that maintain that particularism is a holdover from a premodern past. Here, universalism and particularism exist side by side. In other words, the dissimultaneity of simultaneities has become perceptible. The time of the nation-state (history) is no longer coextensive with the time of the citizen of that state, which results in a breakup of the nation's linear chronology. People are increasingly constructing their biographies without regard to the prescribed rules of the state. This can appear in the form of family time or work time. More important for our argument is the fact that experiences, including local ones, are also oriented toward a global horizon. This, of course, is not a homogeneous time, since globalization is a process of internalization that revolves around the local appropriation of global values rather than a mere superimposition of the latter on the former, as some scholars of homogenization would have it. There are a number of ways to find a fitting system of reference. One can turn inward to one's own ethnic or religious group or look outward to global value systems such as human rights. The time of the nation-state is thus undermined both from within and from without.

Ultimately, the human rights regime both reflects and contributes to the cosmopolitanization of sovereignty on a number of fronts. We have shown that cosmopolitanization finds its expression in a memory imperative commanding the necessity to acknowledge the Other and a critical engagement challenging more exclusionary and heroic modes of nationalism. Liberal democracies are expected self-consciously to engage with memories of past failures and treat them as a standard for political action. To be sure, there is no shortage of states committing human rights violations and, for that matter, also resisting the memory imperative. But they do so at their own peril, and with a cost to their international credibility and sometimes even their sovereign legitimacy. Where liberal democracies are willing to remember past human rights abuses, the nation-state is being revalued in an emerging global memoryscape. This development can be reduced neither to the persistence nor to the demise of nationalism, but it reveals how the national itself is negotiated through the increasingly prominent prism of mnemonic practices that stress postheroic narratives and human rights idioms. Our main interpretive point here is not the emergence of some kind of unified memory, but rather a set of globally shared memory practices.

This is why the difference between what is being remembered and who is remembering remains especially important, given that the consolidation of a memory imperative about past human rights abuses is not a linear, let alone a universal, development. We have addressed the historical formation of the human rights regime with a cosmopolitan methodology that recognizes that the successful diffusion of global norms depends on their vernacularization and specific conditions of local appropriation. Mark Goodale talks about the emergence of a "transnational normative pluralism" as a result of which "human rights have become decentered" (2007, 2). Cosmopolitanism comes into view at the interstices between global orientations and particular attachments, designating the emergence of new, denationalized social spaces and imaginaries. Cosmopolitanism thus does not entail a denial of the persistent reality of the nation for social actors. It rather suggests that forms of national closure are a reflexive response to the reality of cosmopolitan identifications and can be understood only if the social scientist adopts a cosmopolitan perspective.

Such a perspective is essential if we are to understand how the balance between universalism (global) and particularism (local) is continuously shifting and how it is in turn transforming the very premises of nation-state sovereignty. Human rights limit the explanatory power of existing theoretical frameworks. Recent anthropological research on human rights and in the field of sociolegal studies provides ample evidence for this cosmopolitanization and the diffusion of human rights beyond the European focus. In a study on Papua, New Guinea, Michael Jacobsen and Stephanie Lawson show how "local communities may benefit positively from a universal human rights regime without having to sacrifice their own cultural particularities. Indeed, a universal human rights regime may, paradoxically, provide the best hope for the survival of small, politically and culturally vulnerable communities. This is especially so in light of the widely acknowledged fact that people (as individuals or as members of particular groups) are most likely to suffer human rights abuses at the hands of their own government or its agents" (1999, 203). What is at stake here is not only the application of human rights principles but a reevaluation of sovereignty, not as a categorical national entity but as a space within which the relative power of groups and their collective self-understanding is addressed.

Adopting a cosmopolitan perspective should also promote a broader acceptance of the fact that the relationship between universalism and particularism is not only not antithetical but frequently mutually constitutive. Questions of political community, legitimacy, and security continue to be of central concern with respect to rights and a sociology of rights. But they can no longer be captured through the national ontology that has long dominated social and political theory. The global diffusion of human rights discourse has shifted the epistemological conditions for its concretization. In this book we have sought to address innovatively the emergence of a human rights regime and the transformation of sovereignty through the prism of memories. Despite enforcement problems, the persistence of human rights abuses, the emergence of terrorism, and other challenges, the human rights regime remains a global presence, transforming nation-state sovereignty by subjecting it to international scrutiny.

Critics often point out that human rights discourse alone is no guarantee against impunity, let alone the end of human rights atrocities (Woodiwiss 2002). Considering the persistence of mass atrocities in different parts of the world, one could easily succumb to the conclusion that human rights are nothing but words. Our approach differs insofar as we have shown how human rights discourse has set the parameters for legitimate sovereignty by limiting state powers, constituting its interests as well as providing various groups with recourse to a globally available repertoire of claims. Anthropological and sociolegal studies confirm the power of human rights discourse. Mark Goodale refers to multiple discursive effects, including the decentering of human rights and the relevance of normativity, "as the means through which the idea of human rights becomes discursive, the process that renders human rights into social knowledge, that shapes social action" (2007, 8). Words matter, in terms of both convictions that drive action and the political price one may have to pay when refusing to adopt the language of human rights. As Somers and Roberts point out in reference to the work legal rights do, "Rights narratives, myths, ideational regimes, and cultural codes—all of which capture the polysemic normativity of rights discourse—are independent variables no less than the more traditional causal suspects of the economy, the state, class structure, and so on. Aspirational rights claims are constitutive and have the potential power to alter institutions, to constitute social actors, and to shape reality itself" (2008, 407). Rhetorical appeals to human rights have become the global currency with which groups pledge their claims. Do they always act preventatively? No, but what would? Suggesting that human rights discourse is mere words and lacks power, given persistent violations of human rights, is akin to saying that the Ten Commandments are not consequential because people continue to commit adultery, steal, and murder one another.

Will there be human rights abuses in the future? Certainly! But, and this is the crux of our argument, it is precisely the repeated failure to protect human rights that, in the context of the cosmopolitan memory imperative, renders them politically and culturally consequential. As such, the proliferation of human rights and the power of their enunciation is a phenomenon of the late twentieth and early twenty-first centuries, initially triggered by reactions to the Holocaust and World War II. We have addressed this dynamic through different portals, including a host of human rights declarations with the UDHR being a seminal text, an event-driven analysis highlighting historical contingencies (e.g., the Holocaust, the Balkan Wars, Rwanda, Darfur) in response to which human rights have received renewed attention in international politics and among political thinkers. Our political sociology pays close attention to outcomes and to how human rights are simultaneously a means to an end (e.g., political legitimacy) and an end in themselves (e.g., a globally institutionalized norm). Through their increasing institutional under-pinnings they are currently embedded in a global horizon of expand-ing rights and diminishing tolerance for their violation. It remains the case, and surely always will, that their strength consists not only in their institutionalization but also in the recognition, prompted by continual reminders of past failures, of their fragility.

Every time a gross human rights violation is committed, it is per-ceived not as evil but as a political failure and as carrying the seeds, at least potentially, of real action. Does it help the dead? No, but what does? Does it contribute anything meaningful for the surviving victims? Oftentimes it does, for responses to human rights violations can set in motion a whole host of retributive dynamics. Therefore, memories of past abuses, which by definition remind us of a failure of the regime, drive human rights remedies and have further raised the cost of com-mitting such abuses. If there is any consolation to be drawn from the recurring horrors of human rights abuses, it is that the strength of the human rights regime is largely derived from memories of its weakness and volatility.

CHAPTER 1

1. By "human rights regime" we mean a system of rule that goes beyond national rule and includes declarations as well as instruments (see Donnelly 1986 for an early use of this term). All translations are our own unless otherwise indicated.

2. "International regimes are defined as principles, norms, rules and decision-making procedures around which actor expectations converge in a given issue-area" (Krasner 1982, 185).

3. For a view that considers cosmopolitanism as the opposite of patriotism, see Nussbaum 2002.

4. The central drawback of collapsing universalism and cosmopolitanism is not merely that it entails a Eurocentric bias, but it also operates with an ahistorical frame of reference that seeks to shape and freeze particular memories of the past into universal standards for the future. Here we face the danger of reifying a phenomenon by rendering a process into a status. This kind of process reduction is particularly visible when the deployment of normative terms implies the replacement of history with linearity, and the stipulation of a singular (or necessary) path toward development, rather than the coexistence of plurality. This highlights the necessity to historicize developments of cosmopolitanization in the context of changing cultural conditions and political contingencies, rather than to delineate categories of cosmopolitanism.

5. Methodological cosmopolitanism points to a new research trend that aims to overcome the methodological nationalism that dominates much of the social sciences (Beck 2001). It establishes a kind of "methodological scepticism" as a vector of research for opening up concepts and methodological principles of modern sociology, most notably regarding the nation-state as the axiomatic unit of analysis. For more details, see the special issue of the *British Journal of Sociology*, vol. 57, no. 1 (2006), edited by Ulrich Beck and Natan Sznaider.

154 NOTES TO PAGES 11-71

6. The debate about the "normalcy" of mass murderers in the political realm has always been part of the controversy with regard to the uniqueness or "normalcy" of the crimes the Nazis committed. This is also true at the more personal level, as seen in the postwar debates about the "normalcy" of Adolf Eichmann (see Arendt 1963).

7. Our distinction draws on a similar pairing proposed by Dan Diner (2003), who distinguishes between *Erinnerungsgeschichte* (memory history) and *Nationalgeschichte* (national history).

8. The intertwining of nationalism and cosmopolitanism and related questions of solidarity have attracted a great deal of attention among social and political theorists. Sociological accounts of this relationship can be found in articles by Craig Calhoun (2002) and Gerard Delanty (1999).

CHAPTER 2

1. Judith Shklar, like Hannah Arendt, was a Jewish refugee who went to the United States. Shklar's thinking is also shaped by the breakdown of an orderly world.

CHAPTER 3

1. For an in-depth critique of this methodological nationalism, see the aforementioned articles on cosmopolitanism in a special issue of the *British Journal of Sociology*, vol. 57, no. 1 (2006).

2. Schmitt's agenda was to show that all modern political concepts are actually theological (such as the transition from the sovereignty of God to that of the state), whereas Agamben's agenda is to reveal the liberal state as a sham. Clearly these are not contradictory claims.

CHAPTER 4

1. See http://www.armenian-genocide.org/keyword_search.Crimes+against+humanity/Affirmation.160/current_category.7/affirmation_detail.html.

CHAPTER 5

1. There has been recent academic interest in Jaspers's role in West Germany's new postwar identity. In particular, see Benhabib 2006; Diner 1997; Fine 2000; Moses 2007; Olick 2005; Rabinbach 2001; Sznaider 2007.

2. This was also connected to a new form of citizenship that in German is called *Verfassungspatriotismus* (constitutional patriotism), which basically suggests identification with the nation through procedural associations rather than ethnic membership.

This, of course, is completely taken for granted in the United States, but it constituted a reversal of fortunes for Germans. The term was coined by the German political scientist Dolf Sternberger (1979) and popularized by Jürgen Habermas.

3. Article 8 of the constitution of the International Military Tribunal states, "The fact that the Defendant acted pursuant to order of his Government or of a superior shall not free him from responsibility, but may be considered in mitigation of punishment if the Tribunal determines that justice so requires." See http://avalon.law.yale.edu/imt/imtconst.asp (accessed May 15, 2009).

4. Even the film showing the concentration camps, screened during the proceedings, hardly mentioned the word Jew. The prisoners were human beings; the acts the Nazis committed, "atrocities" (Douglas 2001).

5. A. S. al-Khasawneh and R. Hatano, "The Realization of Economic, Social, and Cultural Rights," preliminary report prepared for the UN Economic and Social Council, http://www.unhchr.ch/Huridocda/Huridoca.nsf/0/683f547c28ac785880256766004ec def?Opendocument (accessed January 1, 2010).

6. "Trial of the Major War Criminals Before the International Military Tribunal: Nuremberg, 14 November 1945–1 October 1946," vol. 1, p. 11, http://www.loc.gov/rr/frd/Military_Law/NT_major-war-criminals.html.

7. Lemkin has also been the center of attention in recent studies on genocide. See, for example, Bartov 2000; Ignatieff 2001a; Moses 2004; Power 2002; Rabinbach 2005; Shaw 2007; Stone 2005.

CHAPTER 6

1. Shklar is representative of a rather large group of intellectual cold warriors, including Karl Popper, Isaiah Berlin, and others (see Müller 2008).

2. The strong ideological dimension of this division persists today, as evidenced by the fact that the United States continues to refuse to ratify the ICESCR, while being a vocal proponent of the ICPCR.

3. For a list of the signatories to the main UN human rights conventions as of July 2006, see http://www2.ohchr.org/english/bodies/docs/status.pdf. For a detailed breakdown of signatories to additional human rights treaties as of January 1, 2010, see http://treaties.un.org/Pages/UNTSOnline.aspx?id=1.

4. For a detailed analysis of the growth of NGOs, see Boli and Thomas 1999. Suffice it to say here that from about two thousand NGOs in 1960 their number rose to thirty-eight thousand in 1996, of which approximately half were international NGOs.

CHAPTER 7

1. The ICC has since been ratified by 105 states (in addition to the initial forty-one countries that signed the Rome Statute, its founding treaty).

2. This is part of a long-standing debate among scholars of international relations, juxtaposing "realists" (e.g., Stephen Krasner) with so-called constructivists (e.g., Thomas Risse).

3. For a comparative historical analysis tracing the iconic impact of Holocaust memories, see Levy and Sznaider 2005.

4. See the report by the Independent International Commission on Kosovo at http://www.kosovocommission.org/.

5. The statute creating the ICC, which became law on July 1, 2002, can be found at http://untreaty.un.org/cod/icc/index.html (accessed January 1, 2010). The preamble emphasizes "that the International Criminal Court established under this Statute shall be complementary to national criminal jurisdictions."

6. As of January 1, 2010, "three States Parties to the Rome Statute—Uganda, the Democratic Republic of the Congo and the Central African Republic—have referred situations occurring on their territories to the Court. In addition, the Security Council has referred the situation in Darfur, Sudan—a non-State Party." http://www.icc-cpi.int/Menus/ICC/Situations+and+Cases/ (accessed January 4, 2010).

CHAPTER 8

1. This is, of course, unsatisfactory for human rights activists and theorists (as it should be). In a recent essay on the ritualization of apologies, Cushman draws our attention to the fact that apologetic discourse "creates an illusory reality where values and ethics seem to matter, but where the dominant reality is banality and secular sin" (2009, 238). Even though ritualized apologies need to come to terms with politics on the ground, they nevertheless have the power to generate new beginnings.

CHAPTER 9

1. The manifesto was originally published on May 31, 2003, in the *Frankfurter Allgemeine Zeitung*. For the manifesto and the ensuing debate, see Daniel Levy, Max Pensky, and John Torpey, eds., *Old Europe, New Europe, Core Europe: Transatlantic Relations After the Iraq War* (London: Verso, 2005).

2. As Habermas and Derrida put it, "For us, a president who opens his daily business with open prayer, and associates his significant political decisions with a divine mission, is hard to imagine" (2005, 10).

3. It is, of course, problematic to homogenize memories through designators such as East and West. Stefan Troebst (2009), for instance, points out that the experience of Communism was fairly heterogeneous. Troebst identifies four distinctive memory cultures: those where the rejection of Communist memories is consensual; those with a controversial engagement with that past; those marked by an ambivalence or apathy vis-à-vis the Communist past; and those characterized by mnemonic continuities, usually in states where Communist elites retained their positions. In the context of European expansion and attendant East-West relations, however, these labels make interpretive sense.

REFERENCES

Acharya, Amitav. 2004. "How Ideas Spread: Whose Norms Matter? Norm Localization and Institutional Change in Asian Regionalism." *International Organization* 58:239–75.

Agamben, Giorgio. 2005. *State of Exception*. Chicago: University of Chicago Press.

Ahonen, Pertti. 2003. *After the Expulsion: West Germany and Eastern Europe, 1945–1990*. Oxford: Oxford University Press.

Albrow, Martin. 1996. *The Global Age*. Stanford: Stanford University Press.

Alexander, Jeffrey. 2003. *The Meanings of Social Life: A Cultural Sociology*. New York: Oxford University Press.

American Anthropological Association. 1947. "Statement on Human Rights." *American Anthropologist* 49:539–43.

Anderson, Benedict. 1983. *Imagined Communities: Reflections on the Origins and Spread of Nationalism*. London: Verso.

Appiah, Anthony. 2006. *Cosmopolitanism: Ethics in a World of Strangers*. New York: W. W. Norton.

Arendt, Hannah. 1951. *The Origins of Totalitarianism*. New York: Harcourt.

———. 1958. "Irreversibility and the Power to Forgive." In Arendt, *The Human Condition*, 236–43. Chicago: University of Chicago Press.

———. 1963. *Eichmann in Jerusalem: A Report on the Banality of Evil*. New York: Penguin Books.

———. 1994. "Organized Guilt and Universal Responsibility." In Arendt, *Essays in Understanding*, ed. Jerome Kohn, 121–32. New York: Harcourt Brace, 1994. (Originally published 1945.)

―――. 2007. "We Refugees." In Arendt, *The Jewish Writings*, ed. Jerome Kohn and Ron H. Feldman, 264–74. New York: Schocken Books. (Originally published 1943.)

Assmann, Jan. 1991. "Die Katastrophe des Vergessen: Das Deuteronomium als Paradigma kultureller Mnemotechnik." In *Mnemosyne: Formen und Funktionen der kulturellen Erinnerung*, ed. Aleida Assmann and Dietrich Harth, 337–55. Frankfurt: Fischer.

―――. 1997. *Moses the Egyptian: The Memory of Egypt in Western Monotheism.* Cambridge: Harvard University Press.

Auden, W. H. 2003. *Collected Shorter Poems, 1927–1957.* London: Faber & Faber.

Bamberger-Stemman, Sabine. 2000. *Der Europäische Nationalitätenkongress 1925 bis 1938: Nationale Minderheiten zwischen Lobbyisten und Grossmachtinteressen.* Marburg: Herder-Institut.

Barkan, Elazar. 2000. *The Guilt of Nations.* New York: W. W. Norton.

Barkan, Elazar, and Alexander Karn, eds. 2006. *Taking Wrongs Seriously: Apologies and Reconciliation.* Stanford: Stanford University Press.

Baron, Salo. 1945. "The Spiritual Reconstruction of European Jewry." *Commentary* 1:4–12.

Bartov, Omer. 2000. *Mirrors of Destruction: War, Genocide, and Modern Identity.* New York: Oxford University Press.

Bass, Gary Jonathan. 2001. *Stay the Hand of Vengeance: The Politics of War Crime Tribunals.* Princeton: Princeton University Press.

Bauman, Zygmunt. 1989. *Modernity and the Holocaust.* Ithaca: Cornell University Press.

Beck, Ulrich. 2001. "The Cosmopolitan Perspective: Sociology of the Second Age of Modernity." *British Journal of Sociology* 51 (1): 79–105.

―――. 2002. "The Cosmopolitan Society and Its Enemies." *Theory, Culture, and Society* 19 (1–2): 17–44.

―――. 2006. *The Cosmopolitan Vision.* Cambridge: Polity Press.

Beck, Ulrich, and Wolfgang Bonß, eds. 2001. *Die Modernisierung der Moderne.* Frankfurt am Main: Suhrkamp.

Beck, Ulrich, and Edgar Grande. 2007. *Cosmopolitan Europe.* Cambridge: Polity Press.

Beck, Ulrich, and Natan Sznaider. 2006. "Unpacking Cosmopolitanism for the Social Sciences: A Research Agenda." *British Journal of Sociology* 57 (1): 1–23.

Beck, Ulrich, Natan Sznaider, and Rainer Winter, eds. 2004. *Global America? The Cultural Consequences of Globalization.* Liverpool: Liverpool University Press.

Beetham, David. 1995. "Introduction: Human Rights in the Study of Politics." In *Politics and Human Rights*, ed. David Beetham, 1–9. Oxford: Blackwell.

Benda, Julien. 1946. *L'esprit européen*. Neuchâtel: Les Éditions de la Bacon-nière, 1947.

Beneš, Edvard. 1942. "The Organization of Post-War Europe." *Foreign Affairs* 20 (2): 237–38.

Benhabib, Seyla. 2006. *Another Cosmopolitanism*. New York: Oxford University Press.

———. 2007. "Twilight of Sovereignty or the Emergence of Cosmopolitan Norms? Rethinking Citizenship in Volatile Times." *Citizenship Studies* 11:19–36.

Berkovitch, Nitza. 1999. *From Motherhood to Citizenship: Women's Rights and International Organizations*. Baltimore: Johns Hopkins University Press.

Bernstein, Richard. 1996. *Hannah Arendt and the Jewish Question*. Cambridge: MIT Press.

Birmingham, Peg. 2006. *Hannah Arendt and Human Rights*. Bloomington: Indiana University Press.

Boli, John. 1987. "Human Rights or State Expansion? Cross-National Definitions of Constitutional Rights, 1870–1970." In *Institutional Structure: Consti-tuting State, Society, and the Individual*, ed. George Thomas, John Meyer, Francisco Ramirez, and John Boli, 133–49. Newbury Park, Calif.: Sage.

Boli, John, and George M. Thomas. 1997. "World Culture in the World Polity: A Century of International Non-Governmental Organization." *American Sociological Review* 62 (2): 171–90.

———, eds. 1999. *Constructing World Culture: International Non-Governmental Organizations Since 1875*. Stanford: Stanford University Press.

Boltanski, Luc. 1999. *Distant Suffering*. Cambridge: Cambridge University Press.

Bonacker, Thomas. 2003. "Inklusion und Integration durch Menschenrechte: Zur Evolution der Weltgesellschaft." *Zeitschrift für Rechtssoziologie* 24: 121–39.

Booth, W. James. 1999. "Communities of Memory: On Identity, Memory, and Debt." *American Political Science Review* 93 (2): 249–63.

———. 2001. "The Unforgotten: Memories of Justice." *American Political Science Review* 95 (4): 777–91.

———. 2006. *Communities of Memory: On Witness, Identity, and Justice*. Ithaca: Cornell University Press.

Bourke, Joanna. 2005. *Fear: A Cultural History*. London: Virago Press.

Boyle, Kevin. 1995. "Stock-Taking on Human Rights: The World Conference on Human Rights, Vienna 1993." In *Politics and Human Rights*, ed. David Beetham, 79–95. Oxford: Blackwell.

Brubaker, Rogers. 1996. *Nationalism Reframed: Nationhood and the National Question in the New Europe*. New York: Cambridge University Press.

———. 2002. "Ethnicity Without Groups." *Archives Européennes de Sociologie* 43 (2):163–89.

Brubaker, Rogers, and Frederick Cooper. 2000. "Beyond 'Identity.'" *Theory and Society* 29:1–47.

Brudholm, Thomas. 2008. *Resentment's Virtue: Jean Amery and the Refusal to Forgive.* Philadelphia: Temple University Press.

Brudholm, Thomas, and Thomas Cushman, eds. 2009. *The Religious in Responses to Mass Atrocities: Interdisciplinary Perspectives.* Cambridge: Cambridge University Press.

Brysk, Alison, and Gershon Shafir, eds. 2004. *People Out of Place: Globalization, Human Rights, and the Citizenship Gap.* New York: Routledge.

Burke, Edmund. 1790/1998. *Reflections on the Revolution in France.* Oxford: Oxford University Press.

Calhoun, Craig. 2002. "Imagining Solidarity: Cosmopolitanism, Constitutional Patriotism, and the Public Sphere." *Public Culture* 14 (1): 147–71.

———. 2003. "'Belonging' in the Cosmopolitan Imaginary." *Ethnicities* 3:531–53.

———. 2007. *Nations Matter: Culture, History, and the Cosmopolitan Dream.* London: Routledge.

Cassin, René. 1971. "From the Ten Commandments to the Rights of Man." In *Of Law and Man: Essays in Honor of Haim H. Cohn,* ed. Shlomo Shoham, 13–25. New York: Sabra Books.

Chakrabarty, Dipesh. 2000. *Provincializing Europe: Postcolonial Thought and Historical Difference.* Princeton: Princeton University Press.

Cheah, Pheng, and Bruce Robbins, eds. 1998. *Cosmopolitics: Thinking and Feeling Beyond the Nation.* Minneapolis: University of Minnesota Press.

Chomsky, Noam. 1999. *The New Military Humanism.* Pluto Press.

Claude, Inis. 1955. *National Minorities: An International Problem.* Cambridge: Harvard University Press.

Cole, Elizabeth. 2003. "Shop of Horrors." *New York Times,* October 21.

Cole, Wade M. 2005. "Sovereignty Relinquished? Explaining Commitment to the International Human Rights Covenants, 1966–1999." *American Sociological Review* 70 (3): 472–95.

Connell, R. W. 1995 "Symposium: Human Rights and the Sociological Project." *Australian and New Zealand Journal of Sociology* 31:25–29.

"Cosmopolitanism." 2007. *European Journal of Social Theory* 10 (1). Special issue.

Cushman, Thomas, ed. 2005. *A Matter of Principle: Humanitarian Arguments for War in Iraq.* Berkeley and Los Angeles: University of California Press.

———. 2009. "Genocidal Rupture and Performative Repair in Global Civil Society: Reconsidering the Discourse of Apology in the Face of Mass Atrocity." In *The Religious in Response to Mass Atrocities: Interdisciplinary*

Perspectives, ed. Thomas Brudholm and Thomas Cushman, 213–41. Cambridge: Cambridge University Press.

Cushman, Thomas, and Stjepan Meštrović, eds. 1996. *This Time We Knew: Western Responses to Genocide in Bosnia.* New York: New York University Press.

Dayan, Daniel, and Eliahu Katz. 1992. *Media Events: The Live Broadcasting of History.* Cambridge: Harvard University Press.

Delanty, Gerard. 1999. *Social Theory in a Changing World: Conceptions of Modernity.* Cambridge: Polity Press.

———. 2003. "The Making of a Post-Western Europe: A Civilizational Analysis." *Thesis Eleven* 72:8–25.

Delanty, Gerard, and Chris Rumford. 2005. *Rethinking Europe: Social Theory and the Implications of Europeanization.* London: Routledge.

Derrida, Jacques. 2001. *On Cosmopolitanism and Forgiveness.* London: Routledge.

Dezalay, Yves, and Bryant Garth. 2006. "From the Cold War to Kosovo: The Rise and Renewal of the Field of International Human Rights." *Annual Review of Law and Social Sciences* 2:231–55.

Digeser, Peter. 2001. *Political Forgiveness.* Cornell: Cornell University Press.

Diner, Dan. 1997. "On Guilt Discourse and Other Narratives: Epistemological Observations Regarding the Holocaust." *History and Memory* 9 (1–2): 301–20.

———. 2003. *Gedächtniszeiten: Über Jüdische und andere Geschichten.* Munich: C. H. Beck.

———. 2007. *Cataclysms: A History of the Century from Europe's Edge.* Madison: University of Wisconsin Press.

Donnelly, Jack. 1986. "International Human Rights: A Regime Analysis." *International Organization* 40 (3): 599–642.

———. 1999. "The Social Construction of International Human Rights." In *Human Rights in Global Politics,* ed. Timothy Dunne and Nicholas Wheeler, 71–102. Cambridge: Cambridge University Press.

———. 2003. *Universal Human Rights in Theory and Practice.* Ithaca: Cornell University Press.

Douglas, Lawrence. 2001. *The Memory of Judgment: Making Law and History in the Trials of the Holocaust.* New Haven: Yale University Press.

Dunne, Timothy, and Nicholas Wheeler, eds. 1999. *Human Rights in Global Politics.* Cambridge: Cambridge University Press.

Durkheim, Emile. 1912/1965. *The Elementary Forms of the Religious Life.* New York: Free Press.

———. 1997. *The Division of Labor in Society.* New York: Free Press. (Originally published 1893.)

Elias, Norbert. 1969. *The Civilizing Process.* Vol. 1, *The History of Manners.* Oxford: Blackwell.

Engle, Karen. 2001. "From Skepticism to Embrace: Human Rights and the American Anthropological Association." *Human Rights Quarterly* 23:536–60.

Esterhazy, Peter. 2005. "How Big Is the European Dwarf?" In *Old Europe, New Europe, Core Europe: Transatlantic Relations After the Iraq War*, ed. Daniel Levy, Max Pensky, and John Torpey, 74–79. London: Verso.

Evans, Tony. 2001. *The Politics of Human Rights: A Global Perspective*. London: Pluto Press.

Falk, Richard. 2000. *Human Rights Horizons: The Pursuit of Justice in a Globalizing World*. London: Routledge.

Feuchtwanger, Lion. 1930. *Erfolg: Drei Jahre Geschichte einer Provinz*. Berlin: Gustav Kiepenheuer Verlag.

Fine, Robert. 2000. "Crimes Against Humanity: Hannah Arendt and the Nuremberg Debates." *European Journal of Social Theory* 3 (3): 293–311.

Fink, Carole. 2004. *Defending the Rights of Others: The Great Powers, the Jews, and International Minority Protection, 1878–1938*. New York: Cambridge University Press.

Flynn, Jeffrey. 2009. "Human Rights, Transnational Solidarity, and Duties to the Global Poor." *Constellations* 16 (1): 59–77.

Forsythe, David P. 2000. *Human Rights in International Relations*. Cambridge: Cambridge University Press.

Fourcade, Marion, and Joachim J. Savelsberg. 2006. "Introduction: Global Processes, National Institutions, Local Bricolage: Shaping Law in an Era of Globalization." *Law and Social Inquiry* 31 (3): 513–19.

Gaddis, John Lewis. 2006. *The Cold War: A New History*. New York: Penguin.

Gellner, Ernest. 1983. *Nations and Nationalism*. Ithaca: Cornell University Press.

Giddens, Anthony. 1985. *The Nation-State and Violence*. Berkeley and Los Angeles: University of California Press.

Gleason, Abbott. 1995. *Totalitarianism: The Inner History of the Cold War*. New York: Oxford University Press.

Goodale, Mark. 2007. "Introduction: Locating Rights, Envisioning Law Between the Global and the Local." In *The Practice of Human Rights: Tracking Law Between the Global and the Local*, ed. Mark Goodale and Sally Engle Merry, 1–30. Cambridge: Cambridge University Press.

Gordon, Niv, and Nitza Berkovitch. 2007. "Human Rights Discourse in Domestic Settings: How Does It Emerge?" *Political Studies* 55:243–66.

Habermas, Jürgen, and Jacques Derrida. 2005. "February 15, or What Binds Europeans Together: Pleas for a Common Foreign Policy, Beginning in Core Europe." In *Old Europe, New Europe, Core Europe: Transatlantic Relations After the Iraq War*, ed. Daniel Levy, Max Pensky, and John Torpey, 3–13. London: Verso.

Hafner-Burton, Emilie, and Kiyoteru Tsutsui. 2005. "Human Rights in a Globalizing World: The Paradox of Empty Promises." *American Journal of
Sociology* 10 (5): 1373–411.

Haijar, Lisa. 2005. "Toward a Sociology of Human Rights: Critical Globalization Studies, International Law, and the Future of War." In *Critical Globalization Studies*, ed. Richard P. Appelbaum and William I. Robinson,
207–16. New York: Routledge.

Halbwachs, Maurice. 1980. *The Collective Memory*. New York: Harper & Row.

Halliday, Terrence C., and Bruce Carruthers. 2007. "The Recursivity of Law:
Global Norm Making and National Lawmaking in the Globalization of
Corporate Insolvency Regimes." *American Journal of Sociology* 112 (4):
1135–202.

Harland, Christopher. 2000. "The Status of the International Covenant on
Civil and Political Rights (ICCPR) in the Domestic Law of State Parties:
An Initial Global Survey Through UN Human Rights Committee Docu-
ments." *Human Rights Quarterly* 22:187–260.

Heins, Volker. 2006. "Orientalising America? Continental Intellectuals and
the Search for Europe's Identity." *Millennium* 34 (2): 433–48.

Heitmeyer, Wilhelm. 2004. *Deutsche Zustände*. Frankfurt am Main: Suhrkamp.

Held, David. 2003. "The Changing Structure of International Law: Sovereignty
Transformed?" In *The Global Transformations Reader*, ed. David Held and
Anthony McGrew, 162–76. London: Polity Press.

Henkin, Louis. 1999. "That 'S' Word: Sovereignty, and Globalization, and
Human Rights, et cetera." *Fordham Law Review* 68:1–14.

Heyd, David. 2001. "The Charitable Perspective: Forgiveness and Toleration as
Supererogatory." *Canadian Journal of Philosophy* 31 (4): 567–86.

Hiden, John, and David Smith. 2006. "Looking Beyond the Nation State: A
Baltic Vision for National Minorities Between the Wars." *Journal of Contemporary History* 41 (3): 387–99.

Hirsch, Marianne. 2008. "The Generation of Postmemory." *Poetics Today* 29
(1): 103–28.

Höijer, Birgitta. 2004. "The Discourse of Global Compassion: The Audience
and the Media Reporting of Human Suffering." *Media, Culture, and
Society* 26 (4): 513–31.

Holmes, Stephen. 2002. "Looking Away." *London Review of Books*, November
14, 3–8.

Holzgrefe, J. L., and Robert O. Keohane, eds. 2003. *Humanitarian Intervention:
Ethical, Legal, and Political Dilemmas*. Cambridge: Cambridge University
Press.

Hopgood, Stephen. 2009. "Moral Authority, Modernity, and the Politics of the
Sacred." *European Journal of International Relations* 15 (2): 229–55.

Horkheimer, Max, and Theodor Adorno. 1944/1972. *The Dialectic of Enlightenment*. New York: Herder & Herder.

Hume, David. 1751/1988. *An Enquiry Concerning the Principles of Morals*. Indianapolis: Hackett.

Hunt, Lynn. 2007. *Inventing Human Rights: A History*. New York: W. W. Norton.

Hutton, Patrick. 1993. *History as an Art of Memory*. Hanover: University Press of New England.

Huyssen, Andreas. 2003. *Presents Past: Urban Palimpsests and the Politics of Memory*. Stanford: Stanford University Press.

Ignatieff, Michael. 2001a. "The Danger of a World Without Enemies: Lemkin's Word." *New Republic*, February 21, 26–28.

———. 2001b. *Human Rights as Politics and Idolatry*. Princeton: Princeton University Press.

———. 2004. *The Lesser Evil: Political Ethics in an Age of Terror*. Princeton: Princeton University Press.

Isaac, Jeffrey. 1996. "A New Guarantee on Earth: Hannah Arendt on Human Dignity and the Politics of Human Rights." *American Political Science Review* 90 (1): 61–73.

———. 2002. "Hannah Arendt on Human Rights and the Limits of Exposure, or Why Noam Chomsky Is Wrong About the Meaning of Kosovo." *Social Research* 69 (2): 505–37.

Jacobsen, Michael, and Stephanie Lawson. 1999. "Between Globalization and Localization: A Case Study of Human Rights Versus State Sovereignty." *Global Governance* 5 (2): 203–19.

Jankélévitch, Vladimir. 1996. "Should We Pardon Them?" *Critical Inquiry* 22 (3): 552–72.

Jaspers, Karl. 1951. "Vom Europäischen Geist." In Jaspers, *Rechenschaft und Ausblick: Reden und Aufsätze*, 233–64. Munich: Piper. (Originally published 1946.)

———. 1963. *Über die Schuldfrage*. Munich: Piper. (Originally published 1946.)

Jeismann, Michael. 2004. "Das zweite Symbol: Erfahrungsebenen von Flucht und Vertreibung." *Frankfurter Allgemeine Zeitung*, March 15.

Joas, Hans. 2003. *War and Modernity*. Cambridge: Polity Press.

Judt, Tony. 2005. *Postwar: A History of Europe Since 1945*. New York: Penguin.

Kant, Immanuel. 1969. *Groundwork for the Metaphysics of Morals*. Translated by Thomas Kingsmill Abbott. Edited, with revisions, by Lara Denis. Peterborough, Ont.: Broadview Press. (Originally published 1785.)

———. 1795/1991. "Perpetual Peace: A Philosophical Sketch." In *Kant: Political Writings*, ed. H. S. Reiss and H. B. Nisbet, 2d ed., 93–130. Cambridge: Cambridge University Press.

Kapferer, Norbert. 1993. "Das philosophische Vorspiel zum Kalten Krieg: Die Jaspers-Lukács Kontroverse in Genf 1946." *Jahrbuch der Österreichischen Karl-Jaspers Gesellschaft* 6:79–106.

Keck, Margaret E., and Kathryn Sikkink. 1998. *Activists Beyond Borders: Advocacy Networks in International Politics.* Ithaca: Cornell University Press.

Kim, Hunjoon, and Kathryn Sikkink. 2007 "Do Human Rights Trials Make a Difference?" Paper given at the annual meeting of the International Studies Association, San Francisco, March 2008.

Kirkbright, Suzanne. 2004. *Karl Jaspers, a Biography: Navigations in Truth.* New Haven: Yale University Press.

Knock, Thomas J. 1995. *To End All Wars: Woodrow Wilson and the Quest for a New World Order.* Princeton: Princeton University Press.

Koh, Harald. 1997. "How Is International Human Rights Law Enforced?" *Indiana Law Journal* 74 (4): 1397–417.

Kohn, Hans. 1944/2005. *The Idea of Nationalism.* New Brunswick, N.J.: Transaction Books.

König, Matthias. 2008. "Institutional Change in the World Polity—International Human Rights and the Construction of Collective Identities." *International Sociology* 23:97–116.

Koskenniemi, Martti. 2004. *The Gentle Civilizer of Nations: The Rise and Fall of International Law, 1870–1960.* Cambridge: Cambridge University Press.

Kramer, Alan. 2001. "The First Wave of International War Crimes Trials: Istanbul and Leipzig." *European Review* 14 (4): 441–55.

Krasner, Stephen. 1982. "Structural Causes and Regime Consequences: Regimes as Intervening Variables." *International Organization* 36:185–205.

———. 1995. "Compromising Westphalia." *International Security* 20 (3): 115–37.

———. 1999. *Sovereignty: Organized Hypocrisy.* Princeton: Princeton University Press.

Krzeminski, Adam. 2005. "First Kant, Now Habermas: A Polish Perspective on 'Core' Europe." In *Old Europe, New Europe, Core Europe: Transatlantic Relations After the Iraq War,* ed. Daniel Levy, Max Pensky, and John Torpey, 146–52. London: Verso.

Krzeminski, Adam, and Adam Michnik. 2002. "Wo Geschichte europäisch wird: Das Zentrum gegen Vertreibungen gehört nach Breslau." *Die Zeit,* June 20. (Originally published in Polish in the *Gazeta Wyborcza,* May 14.)

Kurasawa, Fuyuki. 2004. "A Cosmopolitanism from Below: Alternative Globalization and the Creation of a Solidarity Without Bounds." *Archives of European Sociology* 45 (2): 233–55.

Kymlicka, Will. 1996. *Multicultural Citizenship: A Liberal Theory of Minority Rights.* New York: Oxford University Press.

Lemkin, Raphael. 1944. *Axis Rule in Occupied Europe: Laws of Occupation, Analysis of Government, Proposals for Redress.* Washington, D.C.: Carnegie Foundation.

———. 1946. "Genocide." *American Scholar* 15:227–30.

Levy, Daniel, and Natan Sznaider. 2001. *Erinnerung im Globalen Zeitalter: Der Holocaust.* Frankfurt: Suhrkamp.

———. 2004. "The Institutionalization of Cosmopolitan Morality: The Holocaust and Human Rights." *Journal of Human Rights* 3 (2): 143–57.

———. 2005. *The Holocaust and Memory in the Global Age.* Translated by Assenka Oksiloff. Philadelphia: Temple University Press.

———. 2006a. "Forgive and Not Forget: Reconciliation Between Forgiveness and Resentment." In *Taking Wrongs Seriously: Apologies and Reconciliation,* ed. Elazar Barkan and Alexander Karn, 83–100. Stanford: Stanford University Press.

———. 2006b. "The Politics of Commemoration: The Holocaust, Memory, and Trauma." In *Handbook of Contemporary European Social Theory,* ed. Gerard Delanty, 289–97. New York: Routledge.

———. 2006c. "Sovereignty Transformed: A Sociology of Human Rights." *British Journal of Sociology* 57 (4): 657–76.

Linklater, Andrew. 2007. "Distant Suffering and Cosmopolitan Obligations." *International Politics* 44:19–36.

Lochner, Louis P. 1942. *What About Germany?* New York: Dodd, Mead.

Lutz, Ellen, and Kathryn Sikkink. 2000. "International Human Rights Law and Practice in Latin America." *International Organization* 54:633–59.

MacMillan, Margarete. 2001. *Peacemakers: Six Months That Changed the World.* London: Murray.

Mansfield, Edward D., and Jack Snyder. 1995. "Democratization and the Danger of War." *International Security* 20 (5): 5–38.

Mazower, Mark. 1999. *Dark Continent: Europe's Twentieth Century.* New York: Knopf.

———. 2004. "The Strange Triumph of Human Rights, 1933–1950." *Historical Journal* 47 (2): 379–98.

Meyer, John W., ed. 1989. *Conceptions of Christendom: Notes on the Distinctiveness of the West.* Newbury Park, Calif.: Sage.

Meyer, John W., John Boli, George M. Thomas, and Francisco O. Ramirez. 1997. "World Society and the Nation-State." *American Journal of Sociology* 103 (1): 144–81.

Michnik, Adam, and Vaclav Havel. 1993. "Justice or Revenge?" *Journal of Democracy* 4:20–27.

Minow, Martha. 1998. *Between Vengeance and Forgiveness: Facing History After Genocide and Mass Violence.* Boston: Beacon.

Misztal, Barbara. 2001. "Legal Attempts to Construct Collective Memory." *Polish Sociological Review* 1 (133): 61–77.

Moeller, Susan. 1999. *Compassion Fatigue: How the Media Sell Disease, Famine, War, and Death.* New York: Routledge.

Morley, David, and Kevin Robins. 1995. *Spaces of Identity: Global Media Electronic Landscapes and Cultural Boundaries.* New York: Routledge.

Morsink, Johannes. 1999. *The Universal Declaration of Human Rights: Origins, Drafting, and Intent.* Philadelphia: University of Pennsylvania Press.

Moses, Dirk A. 2004. "The Holocaust and Genocide." In *The Historiography of the Holocaust,* ed. Dan Stone, 533–55. Houndsmills: Palgrave Macmillan.

———. 2007. *German Intellectuals and the Nazi Past.* Cambridge: Cambridge University Press.

Moyn, Samuel, 2007. "On the Genealogy of Morals." *The Nation,* March 29.

Müller, Jan-Werner. 2008. "Fear and Freedom: On Cold War Liberalism." *European Journal of Political Theory* 7 (1): 45–64.

Murphy, Jeffrie G. 1988. "Forgiveness and Resentment." In *Forgiveness and Mercy,* ed. Jeffrie G. Murphy and Jean Hampton, 14–35. Cambridge: Cambridge University Press.

Naimark, Norman. 2002. *Fires of Hatred: Ethnic Cleansing in Twentieth-Century Europe.* Cambridge: Harvard University Press.

Nash, Kate. 2007. "The Pinochet Case: Cosmopolitanism and Intermestic Human Rights." *British Journal of Sociology* 58 (3): 418–35.

Nesemann, Frank. 2007. "Leo Motzkin: Zionist Engagement and Minority Diplomacy." *Central and Eastern European Review* 1:1–24.

Neumann, Iver. 1999. *Uses of the Other: "The East" in European Identity Formation.* Manchester: Manchester University Press.

Nino, Carlos S. 1996. *Radical Evil on Trial.* New Haven: Yale University Press.

Nussbaum, Martha. 2002. *For Love of Country?* Boston: Beacon Press.

Ohmae, Keniche. 1990. *The Borderless World.* New York: HarperCollins.

Olick, Jeffrey K. 2005. *In the House of the Hangman: The Agonies of German Defeat, 1943–1949.* Chicago: University of Chicago Press.

———. 2007. *The Politics of Regret: On Collective Memory and Historical Responsibility.* London: Routledge.

Osiel, Mark. 1997. *Mass Atrocity, Collective Memory, and the Law.* New Brunswick, N.J.: Transaction Publishers.

Paine, Thomas. 1791/1985. *The Rights of Man.* New York: Penguin Books.

Pedersen, Susan. 2007. "Back to the League of Nations." *American Historical Review* 112 (4): 1091–117.

Pendas, David. 2002. "'Law, Not Vengeance': Human Rights, the Rule of the Law, and the Claims of Memory in German Holocaust Trials." In

Truth Claims: Representation and Human Rights, ed. Mark P. Bradley and Patrice Petro, 23–41. New Brunswick: Rutgers University Press.

Power, Samantha. 2002. *A Problem from Hell: America and the Age of Genocide.* New York: Harper.

Preece, Jennifer Jackson. 1998. "Ethnic Cleansing as an Instrument of Nation-State Creation: Changing State Practices and Evolving Legal Norms." *Human Rights Quarterly* 20 (4): 817–42.

Rabinbach, Anson. 2001. "The German as Pariah: Karl Jaspers's 'The Question of German Guilt.'" In *The Shadow of Catastrophe: German Intellectuals Between Apocalypse and Enlightenment,* ed. Anson Rabinbach, 129–65. Berkeley and Los Angeles: University of California Press.

———. 2005. "The Challenge of the Unprecedented—Raphael Lemkin and the Concept of Genocide." *Yearbook of the Simon-Dubnow Institute* 4:397–420.

Radkau, Joachim. 2009. *Max Weber: A Biography.* London: Polity Press.

Renan, Ernst. 1882/1990. "What is a Nation." In *Nation and Narration,* ed. Homi K. Bhabba. London: Routledge.

Reus-Smit, Christian. 2001. "Human Rights and the Social Construction of Sovereignty." *Review of International Studies* 27:519–38.

Ricoeur, Paul. 1999. "Memory and Forgetting." In *Questioning Ethics,* ed. Richard Kearney and Mark Dooley, 5–12. London: Routledge.

Risse, Thomas, Stephen C. Ropp, and Kathryn Sikkink, eds. 1999. *The Power of Human Rights: International Norms and Domestic Change.* Cambridge: Cambridge University Press.

Roht-Arriaza, Naomi. 2005. *The Pinochet Effect: Transnational Justice in the Age of Human Rights.* Philadelphia: University of Pennsylvania Press.

Rorty, Richard. 1993. "Human Rights, Rationality, and Sentimentality." In *On Human Rights: The Oxford Amnesty Lectures,* ed. Stephen Shute and Susan Hurley, 111–35. New York: Basic Books.

Rosas, Allan. 1995. "State Sovereignty and Human Rights: Towards a Global Constitutional Project." *Political Studies* 43:61–78.

Rosenbaum, Thane. 2003. "The Price of Forgiveness." *New York Times,* November 8.

Sassen, Saskia. 2000. "New Frontiers Facing Urban Sociology at the Millennium." *British Journal of Sociology* 51 (1): 143–59.

———. 2006. *Territory, Authority, Rights: From Medieval to Global Assemblages.* Princeton: Princeton University Press.

Savelsberg, Joachim, and Ryan King. 2007. "Law and Collective Memory." *Annual Review of Law and Social Science* 3:189–211.

Schechtman, Joseph. 1951. "Decline of International Protection of Minority Rights." *Western Political Quarterly* 4 (1): 1–11.

Schmitt, Carl. 1922/1985. *Political Theology: Four Chapters on the Concept of Sovereignty*. Chicago: University of Chicago Press.

Scholte, Jan Aart. 2000. *Globalization: A Critical Introduction*. New York: Palgrave Macmillan.

Segev, Tom. 2000. *The Seventh Million: The Israelis and the Holocaust*. New York: Owl Books.

Shafir, Gershon. 2004. "Citizenship and Human Rights in an Era of Globalization." In *People Out of Place: Globalization, Human Rights, and the Citizenship Gap*, ed. Alison Brysk and Gershon Shafir, 11–28. New York: Routledge.

Shaw, Martin. 2007. *What Is Genocide?* London: Polity Press.

Shklar, Judith N. 1989. "The Liberalism of Fear." In Shklar, *Liberalism and the Moral Life*, ed. Nancy Rosenblum, 21–39. Cambridge: Harvard University Press.

———. 1998. *Political Thought and Political Thinkers*. Edited by Stanley Hoffmann. Chicago: University of Chicago Press.

Sikkink, Kathryn, and Carrie Booth Walling. 2006. "Argentina's Contribution to Global Trends in Transitional Justice." In *Transitional Justice in the Twenty-First Century: Beyond Truth Versus Justice*, ed. Naomi Roht-Arriaza and Javier Mariezcurrena, 301–24. Cambridge: Cambridge University Press.

Silverstone, Roger. 2007. *Media and Morality: On the Rise of the Mediapolis*. London: Polity Press.

Simons, Marlise. 2002. "Trial Centers on Role of Press During Rwanda Massacres." *New York Times*, March 3.

Sjoberg, Gideon, Elizabeth A. Gill, and Norma Williams. 2001. "A Sociology of Human Rights." *Social Problems* 48 (1): 11–47.

Smith, Adam. 1759/1998. *The Theory of Moral Sentiments*. Indianapolis: Liberty Classics.

Snyder, Jack, and Leslie Vinjamuri. 2003. "Trial and Errors: Principle and Pragmatism in Strategies of International Justice." *International Security* 28:5–44.

Somers, Margaret R., and Christopher N. J. Roberts. 2008. "Toward a New Sociology of Rights: A Genealogy of 'Buried Bodies' of Citizenship and Human Rights." *Annual Review of Law and Social Sciences* 4:385–425.

Sontag, Susan. 2003. *Regarding the Pain of Others*. New York: Farrar, Straus and Giroux.

Soysal, Yasemin. 1994. *Limits of Citizenship: Migrants and Postnational Membership in Europe*. Chicago: University of Chicago Press.

Stasiuk, Andrzej. 2005. "Wild, Cunning, Exotic: The East Will Completely Shake Up Europe." In *Old Europe, New Europe, Core Europe: Transatlantic*

Relations After the Iraq War, ed. Daniel Levy, Max Pensky, and John Torpey, 103–6. London: Verso.

Sternberger, Dolf. 1979. "Verfassungspatriotismus." *Frankfurter Allgemeine Zeitung,* May 23.

Stone, Dan. 2005. "Raphael Lemkin on the Holocaust." *Journal of Genocide Research* 7 (4): 539–50.

Strange, Susan. 1996. *The Retreat of the State.* Cambridge: Cambridge University Press.

Strauss, Leo. 1955. *Natural Rights and History.* Chicago: University of Chicago Press.

Sznaider, Natan. 2001. *The Compassionate Temperament: Care and Cruelty in Modern Society.* Boulder, Colo.: Rowman & Littlefield.

———. 2006. "Terrorism and the Social Contract." *Irish Journal of Sociology* 15 (1): 7–23.

———. 2007. "The Question of Guilt: Karl Jaspers." *Tel-Aviver Jahrbuch für Deutsche Geschichte* 35:373–79.

Taylor, Telford. 1992. *The Anatomy of the Nuremberg Trials: A Personal Memoir.* New York: Knopf.

Teitel, Ruti. 2003. "Humanity's Law: Rule of Law for the New Global Politics." *Cornell International Law Journal* 35 (2): 355–87.

Tester, Keith. 1999. "The Moral Consequentiality of Television." *European Journal of Social Theory* 2 (4): 469–83.

———. 2001. *Compassion, Morality, and the Media.* Buckingham, UK: Open University Press.

Thomas, Daniel C. 2001. *The Helsinki Effect: International Norms, Human Rights, and the Demise of Communism.* Princeton: Princeton University Press.

Torpey, John. 2006. *Making Whole What Has Been Smashed: On Reparations Politics.* Cambridge: Harvard University Press.

"Trial of the Major War Criminals Before the International Military Tribunal: Nuremberg, 14 November 1945–1 October 1946." http://www.loc.gov/rr/frd/Military_Law/NT_major-war-criminals.html.

Troebst, Stefan. 2009. "Geschichtswissenschaft im postkommunistischen Ost(mittel)europa: Zwischen Vergangenheitspolitik und Erinnerungskultur." *Deutschland Archiv: Zeitschrift für das vereinigte Deutschland* 42 (1): 87–95.

Turner, Bryan S. 1993. "Outline of a Theory of Human Rights." *Sociology* 27 (3): 489–512.

———. 1995. "Symposium: Human Rights and the Sociological Project." *Australian and New Zealand Journal of Sociology* 31:1–8.

———. 1997. "A Neo-Hobbesian Theory of Human Rights: A Reply to Malcolm Waters." *Sociology* 31 (3): 565–73.

————. 2006. *Vulnerability and Human Rights.* University Park: Pennsylvania State University Press.

————. 2009. "Violence, Human Rights, and Piety: Cosmopolitanism Versus Virtuous Exclusion in Response to Atrocity." In *The Religious in Response to Mass Atrocities: Interdisciplinary Perspectives,* ed. Thomas Brudholm and Thomas Cushman, 242–64. Cambridge: Cambridge University Press.

Turner, Jenia Iontcheva. 2006. "Transnational Networks and International Criminal Justice." *Michigan Law Review* 105: 985–1017.

Walker, R. B. J. 1988. "State Sovereignty, Global Civilization, and the Rearticulation of Political Space." World Order Studies Program, Occasional Paper no. 18, Princeton University.

Waters, Malcolm. 1996. "Human Rights and the Universalisation of Interests: Towards a Social Constructionist Approach." *Sociology* 30 (3): 593–600.

Weber, Max. 1919/1958. "Politics as a Vocation." In *From Max Weber: Essays in Sociology,* ed. Hans H. Gerth and C. Wright Mills, 77–128. New York: Oxford University Press.

Wehler, Hans-Ulrich. 2005. "Let the United States Be Strong." In *Old Europe, New Europe, Core Europe: Transatlantic Relations After the Iraq War,* ed. Daniel Levy, Max Pensky, and John Torpey, 120–27. London: Verso.

Woodiwiss, Anthony. 2002. "Human Rights and the Challenge of Cosmopolitanism." *Theory, Culture, and Society* 19 (1–2): 139–55.

Wotipka, Christine Min, and Kiyoteru Tsutsui. 2008. "Global Human Rights and State Sovereignty: State Ratification of International Human Rights Treaties, 1965–2001." *Sociological Forum* 23 (4): 724–54.

Zayas, Alfred Maurice de. 1977. *Nemesis at Potsdam: The Expulsion of the Germans from the East.* London: Routledge.

Žižek, Slavoj. 2005. "Against Human Rights." *New Left Review* 34:115–31.

Zweig, Stefan. 1988. *Die Welt von Gestern: Erinnerungen eines Europäers.* Frankfurt am Main: Suhrkamp.

INDEX

1568154R0

Printed in Great Britain by Amazon.co.uk, Ltd., Marston Gate.